PRANKFURTERS

SLADE DELASTRODE

BIG BEASTIE 🦍 BOOKS

Cover illustration © 2019 by Slade Delastrode
Cover design by Slade Delastrode
Book design and production by Slade Delastrode

Editing by Cindy Beatty
Proof Positive Papers
www.proofpositivepapers.com
cindy@proofpositivepapers.com

ISBN: 9798861037020

Second Revised Edition, 2023

This book is dedicated to
my long-suffering wife, Marta,
who always knew my talents and
creativity would win the day.

DISCLAIMER

The contents of this book are presented for informational purposes only. The author and publisher in no way encourage or condone the reader's participation in the activities presented here, some of which are punishable by law as acts of terrorism in the United States, its territories, and other countries. The activities described can involve substantial risk of injury, property damage, and other dangers. Dangers peculiar to these activities include, but are not limited to sprains, bruises, cuts, abrasions, burns, blunt trauma, broken bones, concussion, emotional harm, heart attack, and death.

CONTENTS

PREFACE

 We weren't boys in the 'hood waving guns from the windows of getaway cars. Far from it. We were lily-white teenagers who were never instilled with a strong sense of what was right and what was wrong—and we would try anything that seemed dicey and exciting. Everyday life in 1980 was dull, and our parents were oblivious to what we did to entertain ourselves. Shoplifting, breaking and entering, building and detonating explosives, perpetrating hoaxes—all of these could be ticked off on our long list of unwholesome activities. We were a terrible teen trio who were the scourge of Yorba Linda, and this is the chronicle of our criminal misadventures and general naughtiness told in eleven humorous short stories. The vast majority of the content comes from handwritten manuscripts I penned just days or weeks after the events and is a detailed account of actual incidents without embellishment. I was seventeen or eighteen years old when the stories were written, depending on the subject. And, there were many subjects. Some of them were downright strange.

I'm Slade Delastrode. I grew up in Orange County, that California bulwark of conservatism where life was safe and squeaky clean. Placentia to be exact. I was doing just fine until I was fifteen. My father was layed off from his position with Gulf Oil Corporation in 1976, and he got the brilliant idea that he should retire and that the family should move to a remote, rural part of Central California. In 1977, I left all of my friends behind and had to start high school again. I was a shy, skinny, pimply sophomore in a hick town where I never made friends and "outsiders" were subjected to every kind of abuse. Eventually, I ran away from home and back to Placentia. I bounced around a number of boarding places, mostly living off the good graces of friends. I even re-entered my high school in Placentia. Then, I caught mono from a make-out session with a cute blonde girl (if only it had been The Clap!) and picked up Hep A from dirty cutlery at Reuben's

Plankhouse* in Brea where I worked as a busboy. I returned home to Central California sick as a dog.

Throughout my adversity, I could always count on my Yorba Linda friends, Virge "Don't Call Me Virgil" Faris and Freddy "Not 'Filipino'" Filipo for encouraging words and plans for future get-togethers. Once I was feeling better, I took the California High School Equivalency Test* and was finished with high school at the age of seventeen. The idea that I should move in with Freddy had been floated at about this time. Freddy's parents were good with it; I think they wanted a positive "brother figure" for their son. Without much ado, I made the move to the Filipo residence in April of 1980. Life was to get very interesting very fast.

Virge's parents were apoplectic over my move. I hadn't told anyone of my plans, and the idea of Freddy and me under one roof meant *two* bad influences for their boys were close at hand (the Farises and Filipos shared a back fence!). Virge was less distressed. He knew Freddy and I would be hatching plans for all kinds of wicked escapades, and he was eager to help make things happen.

I quickly found a full-time job as a display ad artist at a Yellow Pages publisher in Anaheim and had an old car of my own. I was set. I was also feeling long overdue for the kind of fun I had only daydreamed about while I languished in redneckville. Freddy and Virge were champing at the bit, too.

The Filipo residence, April 1980

Freddy was a smallish, pale, and slight kid. Virge and I referred to him as "the albino" in less tolerant days. He was sixteen and still in high school when I took up residence at his home. He had receding platinum blond hair as well as beguiling blue eyes that did well to disguise his intelligence and devious intentions. He was also handy when it came to making things from scratch. Freddy was the brains and main instigator of what we called fun.

Virge was tall and lanky and sported an enviously thick helmet of chestnut hair. He was seventeen and in his senior year of high school. A decent student, with a part-time job and a position on the school water polo team, he gave every appearance of being an upstanding youth. But, he wasn't the sharpest tool in the shed, and I don't recall Virge ever having an original idea for mayhem. Nevertheless, Freddy and I valued him for his enthusiasm and his assistance in the un-doings we were always thinking up. Virge was the "unskilled contributor" of the threesome.

As for me, I was also tall and thin and often sported facial hair. As with my cohorts, I wasn't particularly athletic and was always careful not to get myself into ticklish situations where I needed to perform superhuman feats of escape. Like Freddy, I was an intelligent kid. I was always an exemplary student and had been placed in California's dubious MGM (Mentally Gifted Minor)* program at the tender age of nine. I was also inventive and creative. I was the trio's co-instigator and "skilled contributor."

Most importantly, we all got along extremely well. We all had similar interests, and we all had a great sense of humor. None of us took life too seriously. Not bad kids, really. Just unsupervised and left to our own devices.

To keep things in perspective, Ronald Reagan was just about to be elected president. There was no Internet—home computers had yet to become common household items. For those lucky enough to get in on the ground floor with PCs, 5 ¼-inch floppy disks with a whopping 140 KB capacity were the go-to storage media. Video games were crude 8-bit affairs and parlors of the big console types were a relatively new thing. There were no cell phones or digital cameras, either. Rotary phones that required a phone jack in the wall were still used, as were typewriters. Cameras required roll film. Most cars had ashtrays and manual roll-down windows. The standard consumer-level video media was analog VHS tapes. Music was facilitated by vinyl records, cassette tapes, and to a lesser degree by 8-track cartridges. Punk rock hadn't quite died yet, and New Wave music had just crested on the shores of the USA. Who doesn't know New Wave hits like *Girls Just Want to Eat Dung* and *Everybody Eat Dung Tonight?* Yes, looking back it was a shitty era in a lot of ways. Dark times. We made our own fun, and the city of Yorba Linda was our playground.

At the time, Yorba Linda was a bedroom community without major industry, just service businesses for the residents. It borders the city of Placentia where I grew up. It was pretty quiet and unpretentious compared to much of Orange County. Its halcyon days of citrus production were already long gone, though there was still a rural vibe to the area. There were wild spaces and vestiges of agriculture—even a few small orange groves, including the one on Freddy's three-quarter-acre homestead. Most households were middle- to upper-middle-class, with no particularly old or slummy neighborhoods. Yards were often large, especially by Orange County standards. High-schoolers were bussed out to Fullerton because the city had no high school of its own, and it relied on the Brea Police Department for its law enforcement needs. It also has the distinctions of being California's most conservative large community[1] and the birthplace of former President Richard Nixon. Yorba Linda residents worked hard. And they slept hard. God help them all. This city was in for some nasty surprises.

Freddy and Virge and I were many things: delinquents, punks, sneaks, troublemakers, lurkers, evildoers, hoodlums, thieves, crooks, trespassers, con men, liars, bullshitters, parasites, pot smokers, cowards, pussies, jackasses, twits, fools, dolts, halfwits, dimwits, voyeurs, frustrated virgins, and Presbyterians (okay, Freddy was Catholic). While these monikers were accurate for the most part, more than anything we were just plain *dicks*. Giant, throbbing frankfurters—and pranksters. *Prankfurters.* ▪

The names in the following accounts have
been changed to protect my privacy and wallet.
My personal thanks goes out to the numb nuts
at the Brea Police Department and whoever wrote
California's Statute of Limitations, without whom
this book might further be delayed by prison time.

· CHAPTER 1 ·

RECOLLECTIONS OF FREDDY

 My earliest recollections of Freddy Filipo go back to my first year of friendship with Virge Faris, 1975. Freddy was always "that pesky younger kid" who lived next door to Virge. No matter what Virge and I were doing, Freddy wanted to be there and be part of the action. Of course, three was a crowd when you were thirteen and trying to monopolize a new friend's time and attention. I must admit to spurring Virge into a full-blown anti-Freddy campaign for those simple reasons, and somehow it didn't take much persuasion to convince Virge it was justified. Severing old ties isn't hard when you're young and your crude ability to rationalize enjoys a peculiar lack of conscience. Freddy and Virge had known each other for as long as both had been neighbors, and that went back to their early elementary school years, perhaps as far back as 1969. They had even belonged to the same Boy Scout troop when Freddy was nine and Virge was ten. However, despite a long history of tolerance and fraternization, Virge joined me in various nastiness against Freddy for the better part of the eighth grade once we got the ostracism ball rolling. I suppose it was the dark side of male bonding.

Freddy was a wild kid. A hyperactive little bastard with no common sense. Virge told me that when he and Freddy were in elementary school, Freddy once climbed thirty feet to the top of the poplars in the Faris' back yard. Though the excuse was to get a ball, Freddy straddled the long upright branches at the top of the tree and began swaying back and forth. Eventually, the whole tree was whipping wildly about with Freddy clinging to its highest and most yielding parts. Freddy risked serious injury, presumably to impress his audience and to test his courage (not to mention the tree's tensile strength). Now that I can look back, I believe he was just another angry, rebellious Catholic kid. And, an adopted kid who figured wild experiences were worth getting killed. After all, you have fun, hurt the oppressive adoptive parents if you die, and end whatever suffering that's associated with being adopted and not knowing your origins or why you were given up. But, as crazy as he was, Freddy never did manage to kill himself or even get seriously hurt—if you don't count a broken arm from skateboarding.

In another incident, the preadolescent Freddy scaled Virge's twelve-foot-tall basketball pole, which was part of a chin-up bar setup over grass in the Faris' back yard. Freddy stood on the cross pieces supporting the backboard, catching and sinking shots made by Virge and Virge's younger brother, Jake. Virge's mother was in a chaise longue with her back to the whole scene. As you might guess, the foundation and attachments for the basketball pole were rocked free, and a wide-eyed Freddy rode the thing to the ground. "CRASH!" Virge and Jake looked on with their respective horrified expressions, while Freddy rolled around on the grass clutching a bent leg crying, "Oh, my knee! My knee!" Virge's mom very casually turned to look at the mess and then turned back to her book without saying a word. I imagine Freddy got up and hopped home before Mrs. Faris decided to say anything. Typical Freddy.

The aforementioned anti-Freddy campaign of 1975 started when Virge began to complain of Freddy's stupid and squirrelly antics at Catholic school and Freddy's disrespectful behavior toward his nun-teachers and parents. Freddy was once placed in a closet by a nun after he failed to stop running around the classroom and was sent there again on a different occasion for imitating flatulence. It didn't help matters much when he sampled his classmates' lunches stored on the closet floor.

Once Virge began to make judgments of a moral nature, they were etched in stone. Eventually, we concluded that Freddy would be an appropriate target for mischief. We had condemned him as a brat and pest and all, so Virge and I went to the Filipo mailbox one evening and hurled an egg inside. A week or so later, Virge's mailbox received an egg in kind. We were somehow surprised that Freddy had the balls to return the vandalism, and, naturally, our convictions grew stronger and more hostile—he was as awful as we were, and that was bad!

One day after school, Virge and I were standing on his front lawn when Freddy rode by on his bike. As Virge's street was a cul-de-sac, we knew Freddy would eventually have to pedal back out. We then collected pomegranates, stashed them out of parental view in a low-lying juniper hedge near the street, and waited for Freddy to return. Just as expected, Freddy came pedaling back a few minutes later, shooting us the same wary glances he had traded with us on the earlier pass. But, this time we unleashed a volley of hard-shelled fruit!

Despite speeding up and avoiding a direct hit in the bombardment, Freddy was subjected to a pelting with sticky, staining seeds as the pomegranates burst on the street and sprayed his bike. A portion of one pomegranate stuck in the spokes of his front wheel and spat seeds at Freddy with every revolution (I drew a cartoon commemorating this anyway). It was a great day—a great victory.

Shortly after this incident, Freddy employed a padlock on the gate between the Filipo and Faris properties that had remained open for many years. With this insult, Virge and I decided our movement should have a name, and hopefully one that smacked of a large concerted organization that would not immediately connect with us. Of course, anything done to that gate would instantly link to us. No one else had access to it! It just goes to show how faulty our logic was during junior high!

I had seen a drawing of a "Charon" in an encyclopedia, and it appealed to me. It was a mythical creature with a lion's head and body and an additional goat's head; the tail was two snakes. It looked nasty enough, so I suggested to Virge that we call ourselves the Charon Club. Virge was dubious about it at first, never having heard of a Charon and not being able to pronounce the word when seeing it spelled. But, the Charon Club it was.

Virge and I set about to saw the lock off with a hacksaw one afternoon and were successful with some effort. We left the severed lock on the gate with a note attached. The note had a Charon drawn on it (clearly illuminating *my* involvement) with "Compliments of the Charon Club" written underneath. It wasn't more than two hours later that Virge's mother came to us looking perturbed. She had answered the door to find Freddy sniveling, clutching the ruined lock. After Mrs. Faris presented us our evil little note, Virge was made to apologize and promise replacement of the lock. Though Virge's mom didn't feel empowered to make me apologize too, I did feel some regret (even if most of it was for the indignity of getting caught and being confronted with such clear evidence). The Charon Club bit the dust after only two hours. It didn't even last long enough for us to hatch one more simple scheme. A new record for elitist organizations, I'm sure.

All hostilities toward Freddy were concealed after this, and eventually, they became little more than a grudge. Virge and I had instead turned our energies to a task undertaken by every red-blooded American boy at one time or another—tunneling, the creation of the ultimate secret refuge.

Without parental sanction, we selected the most obscure corner of Virge's back garden area—a three-foot-square spot behind a kumquat tree where few people had ever set eyes, let alone stepped. The excavation site's only drawback was that it was against the chain-link fence that separated the Filipo and Faris yards. If it weren't for orange trees blocking the view from the Filipo's house, we would have been discovered and reported by Mr. and Mrs. Filipo and would never have gotten down the three feet we ultimately did.

Virge and I would do the digging after school before his parents came home from work. But, that didn't mean we weren't discovered by someone right off. Just as we first began to make headway, Freddy got an eyeful of our project, and without consulting us or his parents, he started a pit of his own about ten yards away on his side of the fence. "He's hoping we'll link up with his tunnel!" Virge scoffed.

Though we were still suspicious of Freddy and didn't approve of the unconcealed burrowing so near to our own, this was Freddy's way to make warm and fuzzy all that was previously cold and prickly. He dug furiously, almost putting us to shame. His project would not last as long as ours, though.

Before we knew it, we heard the familiar patent bellow of Freddy's father, Arnie. "Fred-RICK!" he boomed. As Virge and I hunkered down to watch, Freddy turned to see the glaring, shave-headed mass that he called "dad" quickly approaching the unapproved excavation.

"What the hell are you doing digging in your mother's flower bed?" blurted the elder Filipo.

"Flower bed?!" We thought. "This is gonna be good!"

Freddy could only blink spastically and shrug.

"You've got work to do!" Arnie continued. "Why are you digging in your mother's flower bed when you've got work to do?"

"This *is* work," Freddy countered, which was much to our amusement, if not his father's.

"You've got chores to do!" Arnie repeated in a loud tone. "Fill in that hole now before your mother sees it… And do your chores!"

Freddy's heroic attempt at gopherdom was snuffed.

Virge and I soon lost interest in our tunnel once we dug through a foot of troublesome, rock-hard adobe clay and saw no end to the substance in sight. Virge's father, Erwin, found the hole several weeks later and worried that someone would fall into it and break an ankle. It became a compost pit for a short time, and then Virge was made to fill it in. But, this was not before Freddy started a more significant, more extensive dig in another part of the Filipo's orange grove.

Nothing ever became of anyone's tunneling projects. Ever. They all suffered from a lack of tenacity and remained three- to four-foot pits that filled with rainwater in the winter. I suspect that the tailings from Freddy's final attempt sat around so long that they were incorporated into the surrounding soil, making a fill difficult. I know there was a deep depression in the grove for years afterward.

The dirt-mining adventures were my last recollection of Freddy before I moved out of the area in 1977. All was forgiven and forgotten by 1979, and we became friendly during my occasional visits to Virge's place. By the spring of 1980, this friendship precipitated my moving into the Filipo residence.

Much of what Freddy did after April of 1980 I have included in the coming chapters, so separate treatment here under my recollections would be redundant. However, Freddy did have one remarkable talent that might sum up his attitude toward life. Granted, this tidbit is scatological and gratuitous (but funny!), and it won't come up in any other context. This is what is best called *suck-farting*.

One evening, Freddy and I were lounging on our respective beds in the room we shared. In the course of a conversation we were having about toilet matters, Freddy mentioned he could fart on command. Well, being a reasonable person, I stated my disbelief and challenged him to prove his assertion. Freddy then assumed an odd position on his bed under the covers: head down, ass raised. Soon there was the oddest sound—like someone with emphysema taking a raspy, wet breath—a wimpy "poot" followed. I was impressed, once I stopped laughing. "It's better if I do it on the pot," Freddy contended. I could only assume it was "better" with regard to involuntary ejecta, so I urged him to go into the bathroom just outside our room in the hall and do his worst with the door open for me to hear.

What issued forth from that commode was un-fucking-believable! Sucking sounds echoing off the porcelain! Raunchy wet farts! A chain of the most offensive noises ever emitted from a human backside! I was in hysterics… But not for long. Midge, Freddy's mother, rushed down the hall to see what the strange hubbub was all about.

"What are you doing?!" she cried from the hall (no doubt she was sure the activities were very inappropriate as well as un-Catholic).

"Going to the bathroom!" Freddy replied in his most indignant tone.

"Well, stop it and come out of there right now!" Midge demanded.

Alas, that was the end of suck-farting.

Another curious fact is that Freddy had modified his bedroom for a specific purpose perhaps years previous to my moving in. Attic access was in his bedroom's huge hardwood closets, and he had arranged weight-bearing items stored under the hatch to allow a quick climb. Very close to the access hole in the attic was a heating duct to his sister Ginni's room, and Freddy had cut a hole in it so he could look through the register. According to Freddy, his sister hosted a neighbor girl named Robin for swimming once. Everyone in the neighborhood who appreciated beautiful girls (myself included) lusted for Robin. She was a teen model/actress and had a captivating face and body. Of course, Freddy attested to Robin's virtues, as he had *seen* via the air duct portal both Robin and Ginni changing out of their swimsuits in Ginni's room. This was enviable!

I should mention that Freddy may or may not have been thoroughly depraved, depending on how one wishes to judge him. He and Ginni were not related by blood. Both were adopted. I must assume this made any voyeurism directed at his sister seem all right in his mind. With Freddy's urging, I too tried the window of lust and managed to see Ginni nude once. She was ample, but her nipples looked so insubstantial that they appeared to have been lightly applied by airbrush. A real, naked girl. Wow! But what's the deal with the nipples? Is this how the average female nipple looks?

Cheap thrills. Yep, we got your cheap thrills right here. Step on up—literally! Going cheap. Or, was that disappointment? ■

· CHAPTER 2 ·

CONFUSING THE NEIGHBORS

 A day in the life, 1979. It was a hot Saturday in September. It would be another seven months before I would take residence at the Filipos'. Virge and Jake Faris, Freddy, and I were experimenting with a homemade diving bell in Freddy's pool. The bell involved a load of some twenty-odd red bricks in a wire bin, which had a nylon hammock secured to it. A tarp had been placed beneath the hammock and inflated. Freddy had the use and inflation of the device down to a science, but the big weighted bin could have easily scarred the interior of the Filipos' built-in pool.

Freddy's parents were in San Diego for the entire weekend, and even though Ginni and her friends were in and out, we still had nothing to fear for our exploits. Freddy's sibling was almost always indifferent to his activities, saving perhaps a curious smile she gave him when something looked particularly strange or dangerous.

Virge wasn't in the pool. He was suffering from a backache and a swollen toe. The injured toe was thanks to a five-pound oven door weight that fell on it at Marie Callender's, where he worked.

After successfully using the bell several times, exhausting myself to the point of gasping in the process, we deflated the air sack and disemboweled its bricks. Jumping into the pool from the roof of the utility sheds and diving board followed. Virge sat watching our antics, terribly amused. However, he soon became anxious when it got to be 5:30 p.m.

"Shouldn't you get out now?" he asked me. "We'll be late for the movies."

"That's right," I thought. We—or at least I—had to meet my friend Alex Wong at 6:10 in front of the house in Placentia where I had a room. We had made arrangements to see *Apocalypse Now*. I just wanted a little longer in the pool—I managed that. Virge then insisted that we invite Freddy to the movies, as he had been kind enough to let us go swimming.

The Filipo pool area, 1980

Freddy was eager to join us when asked. I also made arrangements to go swimming again after the show, as I still hadn't had enough of the aquatic shenanigans. Jake and I waited for the last minute to get out of the pool and then rushed to the Faris' house where we changed clothes. I left while Virge was in the shower.

At the Betts' (one of my most temporary residences), I grabbed a beer. No one was home but ten-year-old Cheryl Betts. Alex zoomed past my boarding place because I had given him a wrong address number. As he turned around to come back down Belford Avenue, I had to stand on the curb waving my arms to convince him that it was me he had seen on the drive past.

There was an air of trepidation about Alex when he saw me with the beer, but then there was an air of trepidation about Alex in most situations. He was a very short and very slight fellow who suffered an almost constant state of hesitancy.

We were at Virge's again soon, I with the beer in hand. I was aware that the Farises would disapprove of my carrying a beer, so I placed the can in the street under Alex's car. We entered, and I introduced Alex to Virge's parents, who were displaying an odd over awareness. I then looked to Virge who was busy digesting the interior of a newspaper.

"Didn't you say *Apocalypse Now* was playing at Brea Plaza?" Virge asked.

"Yes," I replied.

An embarrassing scene followed—just short of hair pulling and kicks to the groin. *Apocalypse Now* was playing exclusively in Hollywood. Once everyone had gotten over my confident but faulty recollection of where the desired film could be found, we all settled for *The Amityville Horror* (which Virge and I had seen together previously). It was a double feature with another film, entitled simply *H.O.T.S.*.

Virge drove. I thought Alex was going to drive, but what did I know?

At the parking lot of the Brea Plaza and its nearby movie theater complex, I paid Virge a past debt by giving him his $3.50 admission in quarters. By a quirk of fate, I would later get it all back.

While we were walking toward the theater box office, a door flew open on the side of the building.

"Virge!" cried a red-suited usher after staring at our crew for a moment.

"Todd!" piped Virge.

The two talked briefly, and then Todd inconspicuously wagged a thumb toward the open door and mumbled, "Go in!" Virge, Freddy, and Alex didn't comprehend at first. They weren't hip to beating the system… yet.

"What?!" asked Virge in a quiet and perplexed tone.

"Go on in!" Todd said emphatically. "Theater one!"

"Thanks a lot!" Virge bellowed, unmindful of the people in a long line at the nearby theater doors.

What dirty looks we got as we slank through that exit door—especially from a big man with his six kids and wife. Virge now gave me my quarters back. He couldn't abide carrying around so much loose change.

H.O.T.S., an R-rated comedy, was a tasteless sexploitation film that might have had the substance of a cartoon or a bad Walt Disney thriller if it hadn't been for all the women's naked breasts. *The Amityville Horror* was better, if only because it enabled me to crack up the rest of the group at tense moments:

"Do you know why there are so many flies in this house? It's because the previous owner was a tailor!"

We left right after the *Horror* and went to Virge's. Alex had to leave—he was running late, and presumably caught it from his parents when he got home. I *thought* I had seen him shaking more than usual.

When Virge told his mom and dad about his friend, Todd, and Todd's money-saving kindness, Virge's father replied with an unexpected smile:

"There's nothing wrong with crashing a movie now and then!"

We then went to Freddy's, young Jake, too, which was surprising, as it was 11:30 at night. As before, Virge didn't swim. But, Jake, Freddy, and I did. We did jumps from the roof of Freddy's utility rooms—dives too, but they hurt and were rather intense. Freddy even threw in a massive mat of foam rubber, and when portly Jake jumped off the roof onto it, he cut a neat hole straight through.

Shortly after midnight, Virge made it known that it was time to drive me home. I quickly exited the pool and whispered to him about the note I had left for the Betts. The note said I was spending the night at Freddy's. Virge caught on:

"Ohhh! Are you guys sneaking out tonight?!"

That was the case. Freddy and I had been plotting since earlier that day. When would Freddy's parents ever be gone for an entire weekend again?

This was an opportunity that couldn't be missed. Jake, who was in the pool, was curious as to why I had quickly confronted Virge with a private conversation outside of the pool.

"Are you guys going to sneak out?!" he asked.

"No!" I lied, "Alex Wong will be back to pick me up in a little while!"

Jake was not to know of such activities. We feared that it would corrupt him, or that his knowledge of such endeavors would create some additional risk where discovery by the adult forms of the Faris clan were involved. With Virge's urging, Jake eventually went home.

Virge entered his back yard through the gate in the chain-link fence between the Faris and Filipo properties a few minutes later. He began having a loud, hypothetical conversation with me within earshot of his parents inside. He even walked through the house, confronting his parents with, "I'm taking Slade home now," to which his mother replied, "All right, but don't be too long." Virge then 'drove me home' by parking at the bottom of Freddy's orchard on Rose Drive. He came up the driveway and made the final arrangements with Freddy and me for a 2–2:30 a.m. meeting in front of Freddy's garage. He then left with some haste.

It was now 12:35 a.m., and Freddy and I were again messing about in the pool. Ginni's innumerable friends, who had been partying in the house while we swam, were leaving now. The fact that Ginni's boyfriend would spend the night made little difference to our plans. After all, presuming that they even cared, they would be busy making the two-backed beast*.

Freddy and I got out of the pool. We ate a sickening assortment of donuts, Doritos with dip, and drank orange juice for the next fifteen minutes. We then sat in Freddy's room and continued our bull session on past adventures. (One story still stands out in my mind: he and a kid named Gregg Dewitte breaking the street lights with Wrist Rocket* slingshots on Rose Drive.)

At 2 a.m., Freddy and I began playing with a propane torch in the garage, melting a 7Up bottle. Shortly after the bottle succumbed to the heat and burst, a slow-moving, bleary-eyed Virge appeared at the back door of Freddy's garage with a handful of aluminum cans and some string on a dowel. Without further ado, Freddy busied himself with tying three cans at regular intervals on the first three feet of line. We then boogied down to the bottom of his driveway.

The long driveway to Freddy's house, 1980

I was a little bit confused. I knew what Virge and Freddy were doing, but why hadn't they told me that they arranged this trick? My two cohorts took the cans on the string across Rose Drive, then gleefully ran back to the driveway to tie more cans on the other end. Virge "ran" in a slow, deliberate fashion, favoring his good toe. I knew if we had to flee from an angry motorist, Virge was screwed.

Headlights soon appeared. A northbound car! Perfect! With Freddy on the far side of the street and Virge and I on the driveway, we raised the string to grille level. The cans whisked out of our hands with blinding speed. A tumultuous aluminum concerto followed. The car went two blocks to Bastanchury Road, where the driver stopped and took off the cans. For the next half hour or so, we enjoyed the sounds of other vehicles becoming entangled in the discarded device.

Mostly unimpressed with the can-and-string trick, we busied ourselves with hurling oranges at cars. This activity was an old practice that was long known as "thrapping," the name somehow being derived from the sound an orange made when it struck a car. Cars in the lanes farthest from us were preferred. We felt they were less likely to see us or discover the launching site at the opening to Freddy's driveway, which was hidden in the shadows of a thick border of pines.

Virge didn't thrap because his back hurt. He would have to watch all the fun. Our first hit led to nothing; we scored one shot on a pickup. Then, right after the pickup, Freddy and I both hit a van. Hard.

"Fwoomp!" "Whup!"

Though it took a while for the driver to make a synapse, he pulled over a block down the road.

"Hey! Fuck you!" the greasy long-haired dupe screamed. "Wait'll you get your own car! Fucking dicks!"

Having said his piece, the unsavory character made an impromptu search for dents from the "rocks"—perhaps finding a splat mark. Freddy seemed to enjoy this little scene (damn him!). He was always so confident and smug and always so surprised when anyone showed signs of becoming a retaliatory threat!

That was enough thrapping excitement for the evening as far as I was concerned. Luckily, we decided to go on to our next matter of business.

Earlier, when we were preparing the cans-on-a-string in the garage, I had told Virge about a small cache of fireworks Freddy had. Of course, Virge's eyes lit up like Roman candles!

The three of us collected Freddy's arsenal and trekked across Rose Drive. We walked through the skeletons of two new half-built houses and into the dark shadows of the line of enormous eucalyptus trees just beyond. The eucalyptus trees bordered the bike trail. We went down the bike trail about a block to Prospect Avenue and then on to the next intersecting street, which bordered a large horseback riding facility. There, we made detailed plans on how to escape our next attack.

Freddy and I snuck up to a nearby house, which faced the street and our position on the bike path. Freddy planned to simultaneously light off two firecrackers and a Ground Bloom Flower on a driveway there, which was to be done by twisting the firecracker fuses to the Bloom Flower's fuse and lighting them all at once. Virge was well down the bike trail, and I only stayed with Freddy until he positioned the fireworks. Freddy and I could  hear a television inside the targeted house from where we stood, and I was not feeling too radical* on this particular occasion. Freddy lit the combo but somehow came away with the unlit firecrackers in his hand. The Ground Bloom Flower went off with its usual whir and blinding light, but nothing more happened.

We walked back down the trail toward Prospect, apprehensive of silhouettes in another house's illuminated window. We then came to the sprawling lawn belonging to a big house on the corner of the bike trail and Prospect. Freddy again used the same fireworks combination but threw it at the house from the street while Virge and I milled about on the bike trail. The explosives snuffed out on connecting with the porch, and Freddy was soon noisily searching in some bushes for them. Amazingly enough, he found the two firecrackers! He lit them, set them down, and ran!

Here's Virge on Freddy's driveway where many a thrapping campaign was launched.
Note the abundance of orange trees. This photo was taken from beneath
the giant Canary Island pine we often climbed to get a commanding
view of the neighborhood (1981 photo).

"BANG! BANG!"

No reaction.

Frustrated, Freddy then un-pocketed a Ground Bloom Flower, lit it, carefully waited for the fuse to burn close, then threw it. The projectile went off in midair and veered away, flying in a lazy loop under its own power. Unfortunately, it fell into the gutter, spent, so we left.

On unanimous agreement, we went off the bike trail through a narrow passage to Rose Drive Elementary School. Much to our surprise, the gate

Front: plastic Piccolo Pete powder capsule; Center (left to right): Piccolo Pete, stripped Piccolo Pete paper powder capsule, Ground Bloom Flower; Back: Pinwheel (all are the 1980 versions)

on the chain-link fence there was unlocked. We eased through, shuffling to the far field of the school, Virge staying well behind due to his toe. While crossing the area, a form darted across the grass perhaps fifty yards away. It stopped us in our tracks.

"It's a coyote!" blurted Virge.

No. It had to be one of those loose dogs that crapped on the fields for the unsuspecting feet of the students. It was indeed a dog, and it dashed off on seeing us.

The bordering houses now sat before us. Only a six-foot cinder block wall separated them from our evil plans, and a bright light in someone's living room beckoned to Freddy and me. I told Virge to

The back gate to Rose Drive Elementary School (1979 photo)

go back to the school buildings so as not to be caught in the open, should we have to escape. Freddy and I then approached the wall where we could see the light—someone inside the house was watching TV.

Freddy lit a Flower and threw it onto the landing at the back door while I was taking my first strides toward safety. Suddenly, there was a familiar whir and a cascade of whirling sparks. Looking back over my shoulder, I saw the house glowing in supernatural splendor.

A porch light immediately went on.

I reached Virge's hiding place behind a classroom on rubbery legs, giggling to myself. We then worked our way back toward our escape gate to the bike trail, Freddy randomly chucking lit Flowers into people's back yards as we went.

"Good Lord!" I thought. "This looks like a 4th-of-July block party!" The houses shimmered like a colossal string of Christmas lights.

By now, Freddy was worked up into a lather. His attacks were now downright flagrant—no doubt to make up for his earlier frustrations at his first failed attempts. Back on the bike trail, Freddy came upon the brilliant idea of throwing lit Ground Bloom Flowers into horse corrals bordering our escape route. I couldn't appreciate the ramifications at the time. Freddy's first victim ran whinnying behind its barn at the offset of the firework. The second horse I only heard—I was in a nervous lead of its antagonist. Virge soon caught up with me, and said with a lilt in his voice, "Oh! That horse made so much noise! It fell on its side and was kicking its legs!" I wouldn't have been amused if I had known the horse might have croaked from its intense fear.

We moved out of the area quickly after this, and soon we were back on Freddy's driveway—just in time to hear a woman's shrill cries on discovering the fallen horse! Freddy and Virge listened momentarily but were quick to dismiss the results of our little game. They also gave me little time for concern. Flush with the moment, we were immediately probing Freddy's trees, getting oranges to throw.

Then, a squad car zipped past. It stopped at the bike trail entrance less than half block away, and with a little navigation squeezed through the two wooden posts there and sped up the trail. (We had been on that trail only a few minutes ago! What if we'd been just a little slower?) Within three minutes, another squad car bisected the area. Dicks that we were, Freddy and I ran for his bottle rockets. A few minutes later, under Virge's protest, we taunted the cops with our whereabouts by launching two bottle rockets from a hand-held contraption made out of antenna tubing with a metal jar lid as a blast plate.

"SSSsssh-POP!"

"SSSsssh-POP!"

Fortunately, nothing happened.

It was now approximately 4:00 a.m. We were straining tired eyes at a light beyond the stand of eucalyptus along the bike trail. We thought it was the lights of a police car, but it turned out to be a street light. A "nodding-bird"* oil pump, heaving up and down, passed between us and the light, making it appear to blink. All was quiet. Then, we heard the noise.

"Pung! Pung! Pung!"

It sounded like someone striking the basketball poles down at Rose Drive Elementary School with a metal baseball bat. We took a fancy to such an oddity and cautiously walked down Rose Drive to the parking lot of the Baptist church next to the school. The noise had stopped, and we waited, sitting on a low wall there. After sitting for awhile, Virge insisted he smelled pipe smoke, so we hurried back to home base. At Freddy's, we heard the noise again.

"Pung! Pung! Pung!"

Freddy then snatched a set of car keys from inside the house, and we quietly pushed his sister's Toyota Celica down the driveway, careful not to alert her. We were convinced we could find the source of the elusive sound now that we had a car. I drove.

We stopped on Rose Drive to get a bearing.

"Saga!" cried Virge.

We drove the quarter mile to Saga Street and stopped. The noise was now louder.

"Go right—down there!" Freddy demanded. "It's coming from your right!"

We then went down Prospect from Saga, across Yorba Linda Boulevard, farther from the school. We stopped, rolled down the windows, and listened carefully. The noise had stopped again.

"Maybe they're putting up a new oil rig somewhere," Virge groaned.

That was good enough for me. Whatever the sound was, it wasn't as seductive as the idea of sleep at this point. It was now 4:30 in the morning.

We returned to the house, knowing it would soon be time to bid reluctant farewells. Nothing lasts forever.

Back at the garage, Virge was sure he had heard Ginni screaming, "Freddy! Freddy!" but his imagination had gotten away from him. We ate more junk food, talked, and Virge shuffled off for home. Freddy went off to bed, and I crashed on the sofa in the TV room.

What a night! This night topped our list of hair-raising stunts for a long time, but even more convincing of its reality was the long two-and-a-half-mile walk I made back to my boarding place at 9:00 the next morning! ■

CHAPTER 3

A LOAD OF THRAP

 Thrapping had a long and illustrious history for Freddy, Virge, and me. Named after the sound an orange made when it struck a car, it was the sport of throwing oranges at vehicles speeding up Rose Drive in the wee, dark hours of the morning. Our projectiles were traditionally launched from the mouth of Freddy's driveway, which was a spot fairly well concealed by a screen of big pines. And, there always seemed to be oranges, or "scoranges" as we called them, in Freddy's small orange grove. Orangethorpe Avenue even became known as "Orangethrap" or "Scorangethorpe" among the three of us, not because we used the local street for thrapping, but simply because it seemed clever.

What was the "average" thrap like? Well, most direct hits would slow a driver down some, or more spectacularly cause them to lock up the brakes, resulting in a stupendous screech of tires. One time, an orange that Freddy threw went directly through the open driver's window, narrowly missing the driver! Strangely enough, this driver continued merrily on their way without slowing, which was entertaining, but guilt-inducing at the same time. And then there was the ever-present banter:

"*I* hit it!"

"No you didn't! *I* hit it!"

"Did you hit it?"

"Nobody hit it."

"Oh! We almost hit it!"

"Whoa! We *both* hit it!"

Our nocturnal sport didn't go unreported, either. More than once, the cops whizzed past the Filipo's property, suddenly flashing on their blinding spotlight. They would do this as much

The humble Valencia orange, our weapon of choice.

Thrapping, anyone? Here's the view from our traditional launching site, just inside the entrance to the Filipo's property. 1981 photo.

as a block before or after Freddy's driveway, not knowing exactly where the assault was being staged. However, I can attest to seeing Virge lit up once while he was at the bottom of the hill leisurely closing the driveway gate after we had wrapped up our activities. Freddy and I were most of the way up the hill and were impatiently watching Virge when he suddenly became an ink-black silhouette in a squad car's spotlight. The cop had switched it on at just the right split second. Happily, that was it. The cop kept going at breakneck speed out of the area. He had better things to do than bust orange-throwing punks, I guess. There were murderers and rapists and Bunco parties out there, somewhere. Lucky us.

Of course, the Filipo orange grove had to be harvested at some point. It was a money-making affair for Freddy's dad, and Freddy and I were both roped into the picking, crating, and transportation of many hundreds of ripe fruits. The day in 1980 that we took the load of oranges to the distributor, Freddy and I rode in the bed of the old, white behemoth of a pickup truck his father, Arnie, maintained for this purpose. Freddy couldn't resist launching a few scoranges from the truck, but I begged him not to throw them at other vehicles in broad daylight.

We were on a major thoroughfare in Placentia, traveling at upwards of fifty miles an hour. Freddy fired an orange with every muscle and sinew, and the missile cleared two lanes, hurtled neatly through all of the cars in a vast mini-mall parking lot and into the open door of a business! We witnessed it bounce violently off of a counter front before it was out of our line of sight. It was amazing! I screamed "NO WAY!" and we both began to laugh hysterically. The combination of the truck's speed and the colossal throw resulted in something to tell the grandkids! Unfortunately, Arnie also witnessed this stupefying feat in the rearview mirror. We were thoroughly castigated through the little window on the back of the cab.

BAD BEGINNINGS

Thrapping officially began with a really nasty incident featuring a five-foot dirt rise just across Rose Drive from Freddy's grove. There had once been a farmhouse there, evidenced by a narrow driveway with a low stone wall on either side. It was a sunny day in the spring of 1974, and spring meant ammunition from the grove was absent, the trees exhibiting only intoxicating blossoms. Ten-year-old Freddy and eleven-year-old Virge came upon the idea that the dirt clods that were abundant on top of the berm across the street would make suitable projectiles for a new game.

They weren't having much luck and were about to give up when Virge turned to Freddy to tell him that he wanted to withdraw. Freddy was standing up in full view of passing cars with a large chunk of concrete raised over his head. Everything went into slow motion. "Noooo!" Virge cried, but it was too late. The plunging concrete struck the half-open passenger window of a '50s "Classic Car" traveling north in the lane closest to them. "Whumpf!" It sheered off the window and bounced off the passenger seat, landing in the lap of the driver. The car came to a screeching, rubber-burning halt, and Freddy and Virge quickly retreated to the bike trail, which was only a few yards from their position.

"You idiot!" Virge screamed at Freddy. "What were you thinking? That was *so* stupid!"

The two small terrorists made their way up the bike trail to the first intersecting street, Prospect Avenue. They milled about for a while and eventually assumed that the coast was clear. They then retraced their steps the couple of blocks they had covered in their escape. Back on Rose Drive, they stopped momentarily at the bottom of Freddy's hill.

As Freddy and Virge stood conversing, they spied the unmistakable "Classic" crest a rise on Rose Drive, headed south now, straight for them!

"Get in the ditch!" Freddy shouted at Virge.

The closest hiding place was a deep dirt drainage trench that paralleled the street. They immediately jumped in and moved quickly to where the trench terminated at a corrugated metal pipe under El Cajon Avenue. The pipe was too small to crawl through, so Freddy lay with his back against the dirt wall, with Virge hunkering down a few yards away.

The car approached slowly and stopped nearby. Though they couldn't see anything on the road without giving away their positions, the two boys heard the car plainly and were sure it was all over. Their hearts pounded madly in their throats. Within seconds, a man's footsteps were heard approaching the ditch. Freddy couldn't stand the suspense a second longer and launched himself out of the ditch in full view of the angry, middle-aged driver and headed up El Cajon at full speed.

The man snapped his head to look for a split-second at Virge, who was now exiting the far end of the trench, then gave chase to Freddy who was closer, but quickly gaining a lead. Freddy ran two blocks to where El Cajon ended at an open field and had nowhere else to go. The big concrete drainage ditch was on the far edge of the field, but rather than attempt a perilous climb of the floppy chain-link fence that bordered it, he opted to jump into one of many holes in the field—"forts" neighborhood kids had excavated. Once in the hole, Freddy pulled a large piece of plywood over it to conceal himself.

"Crunch! Crunch! Crunch!" The now-familiar footsteps approached the hole. Closer, closer! *Too* close! In panic, Freddy reached up and shoved the plywood backwards off of the hole, striking his pursuer across the ankles. While the man stopped for a few seconds to hop around in pain, cursing, Freddy ran headlong for the drainage ditch, scaled the fence and dropped a painful ten feet to the hard bottom. As he sat in agony from the impact, he looked up to see the man at the fence above him. Still in panic mode, Freddy ran up the drainage ditch to where he knew was another field—the one near Virge's street. Now the real trick! Getting out! He looked around for debris and found an old metal paint drum and some wet, rotted limbs and logs. Leaning these items against the wall of the ditch, he was able to reach the top edge and pull himself to safety.

Freddy and Virge soon met up again and were back in the neighborhood into which Freddy had fled. This time on a side street to El Cajon— Mimosa Drive. They were doing reconnaissance, making sure the nightmare had ended. No such luck! The car magically appeared, turning onto Mimosa from El Cajon. They ran for the two nearest houses, hiding behind a chimney in the narrow space between them. The man in the car cruised up the street slowly, scanning left and right. Turning around at the end of the street, a cul-de-sac, he returned just as slowly, showing no indication that he had seen Freddy and Virge's mad dash between houses.

"Maybe Gregg's home!" Freddy told Virge. "We can hide out there." Gregg Dewitte, a creepy ten-year-old Freddy knew mostly because their properties shared a fence, was indeed home just a couple houses farther down Mimosa. Seeing Freddy and Virge in their agitated state, Gregg let them inside to get the lowdown. The three boys were immediately confronted by Gregg's well-meaning mother.

"Wow! You boys look hot and sweaty!" she said. "What have you been doing?"

"Um, skateboarding," Freddy responded, still breathing hard.

Mrs. Dewitte didn't notice that neither of her visitors had skateboards with them.

"Mrs. Dewitte, can we have some water?" Freddy inquired.

"Sure, Hon," she said. "There's Sparkletts in the kitchen."

Gregg showed the boys to the water cooler when a phone rang somewhere in the house. Mrs. Dewitte scurried off to get it.

"What are you guys doing?" asked Gregg quietly, sure that the details would be juicy.

"Oh! Oh!" Virge began excitedly. "We were throwing dirt clods at cars and Freddy threw a huge piece of concrete that wrecked a car!"

"Really? No way!" Gregg said, agog.

"No, REALLY!" Virge insisted. "It hit this car's window and smashed it!"

Freddy looked pleased with himself as Virge supplied all the details, but his smirk soon disappeared when Gregg's mother reappeared.

"Boys, that was Mrs. Filipo. She says that there were kids throwing rocks at cars and a car was damaged. Did you see anything?"

"No, no," Freddy and Virge lied, fully expecting the boom to be lowered on them right then and there. She continued without the slightest hint of suspicion.

"Well, okay… Freddy, your mom wants you to come home now."

Gregg gave Freddy a knowing, plaque-toothed, sadistic smile.

Back at home, Freddy discovered that the man drove his Classic car all the way up the long Filipo driveway and had made an inquiry of his mom about kids in the neighborhood who might be throwing rocks at cars. Freddy's mom asked Freddy the same question Gregg's mother had, and she got the same answer. She seemed completely satisfied when Freddy added that he had been at Gregg's the whole time. Freddy would always have this lucky knack for dodging bullets.

THE GOLDEN AGE OF THRAPPING

Fast forward to 1979. Erwin Faris was driving Mrs. Faris, Virge, Jake, and me to church during one of my visits with Virge. As he turned out of Loie

Street and onto Rose Drive, a mess of battered oranges and orange shards could be seen all over the asphalt. "Looks like someone's been in the Filipos' grove," Mr. Faris said. He seemed to just be stating a fact and implying nothing. Everyone murmured or nodded in agreement. Virge and I could only look at each other with amused expressions. All of the fragments were testimony to a successful night of thrapping—lots of fruit-destroying impacts. Virge's parents never caught on to the fact that *we* were the culprits—and regular offenders.

It was 2:00 a.m. one summer Sunday in 1980, and Freddy and I wanted to do some thrapping. Sadly, there was a conspicuous lack of suitable "scoranges"—only tiny green ones could be found on Freddy's trees, and though the large green ones made for good throwing, these were just too small.

"How about pumpkins?" Freddy asked.

"Pumpkins aren't in season!" I countered.

"Maybe small ones! I think I saw some vines up the bike trail—let's check it out."

Between Prospect Avenue and Santa Fe Street was someone's long, skinny yard that bordered the bike trail. It always had an abundance of vegetables year-round. Freddy scaled the combination split-rail and chain-link fence and began rummaging through the jungle of plants. After a few minutes, he returned with something odd.

"What's *that*?!" I quietly exclaimed.

"Banana squash!" Freddy whispered with a grin.

The thing was two feet long and as thick as my calf. I was incredulous.

"How can we throw that?!"

"Cut it up!"

"Are there more?"

"Yep."

"Get another one!"

Back at the Filipos' driveway, we cut up one of the enormous vegetables into softball-size pieces with Freddy's big pocket knife. Thrapping commenced.

"X" marks the big yard where we sometimes filched banana squash and pumpkins (1980 aerial photo).[5]

We had trouble with the banana squash (the aptly named *Cucurbita maxima*). Even the smaller pieces were too oddly shaped to get a good grip, and they were slippery after being cut. We just weren't getting the velocity and distance we did with oranges. Freddy suggested that if we were closer to the cars we'd have better luck:

"Look, there's all this space on the shoulder."

He pointed to the street just outside of his driveway where an ancient metal guard rail prevented cars from dropping into the dirt trench there. The guard rail caused the lane to narrow, creating a big triangle of asphalt in the shadows of the pines.

I declined to put myself in additional risk of discovery. The driveway was a lot darker because it was a confined space between the trees on the property line. But, Freddy was always one to add more excitement to his skulduggery, so he squatted in the dark on the side of Rose Drive with chunks of squash at the ready.

A car was coming up Rose Drive, three of its four lanes away. It was an old Chevrolet El Camino. At the perfect moment, Freddy lunged up and forward, pitching his projectile. "SMACK!" A direct hit! Freddy dashed for the cover of the driveway.

The blow to the car didn't slow the driver down in the slightest, and the driver continued up the road until they disappeared over the rise. It was then that Freddy noticed something unusual in the middle of the street. He ran out to retrieve it. It was a saucer-size chunk of the car's plastic grille. Powerful things these banana squash! We kept it as a souvenir prominently displayed on the wooden cabinet top Freddy used as a workbench in the garage.

PENETRATIONS

While the vast majority of our thrapping victims seemed unable to find, or unwilling to penetrate our base of operations, there were a couple of occasions where things became extremely hairball.* The first incident was unrelated to thrapping specifically, but did involve a thrown object.

Because I was in residence at the Filipos' in 1980, there was always something nefarious going on at the bottom of the grove in the wee hours of any given weekend. One summer night, Freddy and Virge and I were

The view of the Filipo's property from the bike trail. The break in the line of pine trees marked by the arrow is the driveway entrance, which was difficult to see at night. 1981 photo.

entertaining ourselves with the bottom half of a blue 55-gallon plastic drum that had been filled with water. Gregg Dewitte and one of his perpetually stoned, long-haired friends, Eric, had come by to smoke-out and to watch us throw various lit fireworks into the water to see how they would react. (Ground Bloom Flowers rolled on every axis, both gurgling and hissing as they emitted light, bubbles and smoke. Nice.)

On an impulse, I tossed a lit stripped-down Piccolo Pete through the line of pines that concealed us. It struck the middle of Rose Drive, shrieked, and flew a few feet into the air. It wasn't my sole intention per se, but it landed in front of a northbound pickup truck. The driver slowed to assess the danger for a couple of seconds, and then proceeded on his way. It was no more than twenty minutes later that the same truck reappeared. It pulled over just outside of the tree line and disgorged a gang of perhaps six twenty-somethings in baseball jerseys yelling threats. They jumped out of the bed and cab—with baseball bats!

With only a small chain-link fence and the trees between us and this threat, we instinctively dumped the barrel and scattered through the grove. Gregg and Eric made it to the far side of the lot and hopped the fence, headed for Gregg's house. Freddy, Virge, and I skillfully navigated familiar paths through the grove to the house, where we heard the would-be attackers shouting and thrashing the vegetation inside the property. They never made it as far as the house.

Freddy's parents were deep sleepers. They weren't awakened by much, and this ruckus was no exception. The truckload of testosterone-crazed assholes soon left after finding nothing but the empty blue drum and an assortment of spent fireworks lying in a muddy swath. We figured these characters saw an opportunity for the excitement of committing violence—avenging the affront to their pickup driver friend, and probably instigated by the driver, too. Or, looking at the incident more graciously, they may have wanted to just frighten whoever was wantonly tossing fireworks onto the street. The latter could be called a prank, in which case the pranksters had been pranked (just deserts!). But there could just as likely have been broken bones involved.

The following winter, I was away to visit family for Christmas, and Freddy and Virge made their own fun without me. This included the traditional thrap with over-ripe oranges that had somehow managed to linger on the trees. They were having a good go of it, too. Rose Drive was awash in pulverized oranges.

The two "Counts of Commotion" were close to concluding their festivities when they had a particularly loud and powerful "double score" on a muscle car. The driver laid down fifty feet of smoking rubber in a screeching halt, then proceeded up the street perhaps a block at a very slow speed. Freddy and Virge watched from the mouth of the driveway, only to see the car abruptly make a one-eighty and head back their way. Time to go! They ran up the driveway and were within thirty feet of the house when they were caught in the car's headlights. Their victim had found the obscure entry to the property and was coming slowly and cautiously up the hill!

Virge ran for the gate between his and the Filipos' properties, but stopped short and turned around. He wanted to see what happened next. He hunkered down behind some shrubs to watch. He could hear a string of obscenities from the driver and his equally depraved passenger as they stopped on the flat expanse of asphalt at the top of the driveway.

Freddy had run to the pool area where he grabbed a garden hose. He then scaled the house using the fence around the pool and took a position on the crest of the roof. He figured that if the intruders exited the car, a good cold hosing would drive them away. The driver shouted a few choice epithets, which sounded like parting jabs, but Freddy remained at the ready. Squealing donuts ensued—around and around and around the car went, depositing loop after loop of tire marks in its wake. The invaders were briefly hosed, and to Freddy's astonishment, the car sped down the driveway and disappeared onto the streets with more skidding tire sounds. Just then, he heard a voice from behind him. "Get in the house!" he heard someone say in a hushed voice. "Arnie and Midge are awake! There's lights on!" It was Virge, now crouched on the roof behind him. Virge had been on the roof with Freddy for at least part of the hosing scene. They parted and reentered their homes within minutes, Freddy entering through the door in the garage.

As Freddy passed through the living room, he came upon his father who was poised behind the curtains of a window overlooking the driveway. Arnie was startled by Freddy's sudden appearance, but began to speak to him in a firm, measured tone. He didn't want to cause additional alarm to his wife.

"Fredrick! Where have you been?!"

"Outside!"

"What was all that noise? Were those friends of yours?"

"No."

"Was that you on the roof?"

"Yes."

"What were you doing on the roof? Why are you dressed?"

"I thought there was someone outside, so I got dressed and went out to look!"

Arnie wasn't buying it.

"You've got some explaining to do, young man! But it'll have to wait until morning. Go to bed. NOW. Don't leave the house again."

Freddy was a master at explaining away a nasty incident, mostly by minimizing its every aspect. The car doing donuts on the driveway was just some drunk who mistook the driveway as a street. Freddy had heard the car enter the property long before the donut spectacle, got dressed, and went out to see what was going on. He got on the roof and took the hose with him to discourage any additional encroachment, which proved to be necessary. He drove off the intruder. His mom and dad should be proud of him.

Arnie and Midge weren't exactly "proud" of Freddy's professed heroics, but though his story wasn't iron-clad, it sounded plausible enough that his parents let the whole thing slide relatively quickly. Explaining the fruit-a-licious carnage Arnie was to discover on Rose Drive was the next challenge for Freddy.

"Look at this mess! Damn these kids!" Arnie cursed as the family left for Mass the next morning.

"This happens *a lot*. Fredrick, do you know the kids who are doing this?"

"No," answered Freddy, plainly annoyed.

"No one talks about it at school?"

"No. I get bussed to a school in a different city. No one knows what goes on around here."

Then came the all-important question that for so many years had never been asked before.

"Did you and Virgil do this?"

"No," responded Freddy, his heart ticking up.

"Are you *sure* it wasn't you and Virgil?"

"No! And how could I be *sure* it *wasn't* me and Virgil?! That doesn't make any sense!"

"Okay. We won't talk about this anymore. But, I'm going to watch this situation. It's really ticking me off!"

When I returned to the Filipos' after my winter holiday, Freddy and Virge told me about the incident with the hooligans on the driveway. I was aghast. Freddy also let me know that the jig was up where thrapping was concerned. We were confounded. How could we *not* leave a trace after a successful night of thrapping—it was a patently untidy affair. Virge still had enough enthusiasm for the sport that he suggested we clean up the road afterward, but this was preposterous, and all I could do was laugh at the thought of us collecting hundreds of pieces of sticky fruit-crap. Yep, Arnie and Midge were onto us somehow. Thrapping suddenly bit the dust like the oranges that met their fates out on Rose Drive. ▪

· CHAPTER 4 ·

SLADE NEEDS A STEREO

 Freddy and I had sticky fingers. No, not from frequent masturbation (though this was the extent of our sex lives), but a propensity to *steal*. Whenever we had a project that required small components, or whenever we simply wanted a kick, we were off to a favorite retail establishment for the "five-finger discount." We lifted pipe fittings from a local hardware store to make bongs out of shampoo bottles. When we wanted clothes, we would go to the Brea Mall or Miller's Outpost,* select what we wanted, enter a dressing room, put everything on under the baggy clothing we wore into the store, and then just walk out, grinning. We had a knack for it, and we had stupendous luck!

Shoplifting ultimately became a competition between Freddy, Virge, and me once Virge was introduced to the practice. Books, batteries, hand tools, small household articles. It didn't matter. Whoever could come home with the most audacious and pricey items. Of course, Freddy was the one to do the riskiest snags.* He had the biggest balls and the most devil-may-care attitude about pinching stuff. As our hoards of ill-gotten goods accumulated, we simply told the parents that we had bought them with our own money. After all, Virge and I had proper jobs. As for Freddy, he would say they were given to him by

friends, or that he found them cheap at garage sales. It depended on what was in question. It was never a problem.

Powerful, aftermarket car stereos and speakers were all the rage in the early 1980s. Obnoxious drivers, their windows down and blasting the shittiest music available on cassette tape were commonplace. I had a wimpy factory-installed AM/FM radio in my '72

Caricature of Freddy by the author (1980)

Corolla and offhandedly mentioned to Freddy that a nice sound system in my car would make our frequent trips around town more fun. He filed this away somewhere in his gray matter and decided to surprise me with a free stereo when he had the opportunity to purloin one.

Freddy went down the bike trail alone one night, perusing vehicles in the neighborhoods along our traditional highway and escape route. Between Prospect and Valley View Avenues, he came upon a big, empty lot between the trail and Rustic Road, a spur off of El Cajon Avenue which terminated in a cul-de-sac. There were houses on either side, but the residents had taken to parking their wheeled excess on the dirt lot. He dropped his ten-speed, hopped a low split-rail fence, and walked among the few cars there, testing the door handles as he went. The first two vehicles were locked up tight. Then he tried the last car, a black Ford Maverick. "Click!" The driver's door was open. Just then, the front porch light came on at the house bordering the lot to the southeast. Freddy retreated to the bike trail and watched to see if anyone would appear. After waiting for a

"X" marks the spot where Freddy found his prey— a dirt lot just off the bike trail where residents parked their cars (1980 aerial photo).[5]

few minutes and seeing no more activity at the house, he approached the Maverick and opened it. Score! There was an in-dash aftermarket stereo. It was nothing fancy, but there were speakers in the front doors and on the back deck, too.

The fact that the stereo was mounted in the dash was a problem. Freddy was confident in his ability to use the few tools he had brought with him, but getting to his prize would take time. He eased into the car and unlocked all the doors in case he needed to make a quick escape. He then quietly shut the driver's door behind him and began probing around under the dash using a penlight and a Phillips-head screwdriver. The stereo itself would have to wait. There was no obvious way to access it.

Freddy had been hunkered down in the Maverick for about twenty minutes removing the door speakers when he heard the front door of the nearby house slam. He stayed out of sight below the dash and listened carefully.

"Gwuf, gwuf, gwuf."

Footsteps!

"Gwuf, gwuf, gwuf."

They were coming in his direction, and they were getting close!

"GWUF, GWUF."

The footsteps stopped somewhere near the car. Was it the owner? Did the owner have an inkling that something was up? Freddy had to make a decision—and fast! Should he launch a hasty escape, or see what happened next? He waited five full, painful minutes.

The footfall began again, but this time it was toward the house. Freddy slowly lifted his head until his eyes cleared the dashboard. He could see a young man entering the house. Strange. This guy didn't seem to be worried about anything, so Freddy went back to his task.

The wires from the speakers disappeared under the back of the dash. He might as well start disassembling it. There was nothing straightforward about it, either. Freddy put the penlight between his teeth and unscrewed every screw he could find. After thirty minutes he was making decent headway. He realized that a couple of tabs secured the whole thing, and with some lifting and pushing the console was loose.

The door of the house opened and slammed again.

"Gwuf, gwuf, gwuf."

The footsteps returned, this time stopping closer to the Maverick. Again, Freddy waited. The man shuffled around the car, but didn't open a door or look through the windows, and again withdrew to the house. Doubly strange.

Back to work. The dash was not completely free. Freddy had difficulty seeing behind the loose dashboard and he was in a conspicuous position as he tried to wrestle a view. He finally discovered that he had to disconnect the speedometer cable and the wiring connector before removing it. Now the console was off, and Freddy began to dig through new wires he had uncovered. Which one went to the stereo? Things were still obscured by the metal framework the dash had been attached to. He cracked a window to prevent fog that was now forming on the inside of the windshield and went back to business.

"Gwuf, gwuf, gwuf."

The man was back. This time, Freddy smelled cigarette smoke. The guy had been coming out to the lot to smoke and was doing so just outside the car. He didn't have a clue that a major procedure was going on inside. A few minutes passed, and the man trudged back to the house.

Freddy needed to wrap things up. He'd been in the black Maverick for an hour and a half. It was only a matter of time before he was discovered. In frustration, he cut *all* the wires running behind the stereo, yanked it out and moved to the back deck to remove the two speakers there. This effort took far longer than he had hoped, and before he knew it, the smoking man was back. There was nowhere Freddy could go. He simply kneeled stock still on the back seat staring at the dark figure three feet away. He could see the bright cherry of the cigarette bloom and fade, over and over again. The man finally left, still none the wiser.

Success! The whole system was removed! Freddy even came away with most of the speaker wire. He looked around the interior of the car for any tools he might have dropped. The dashboard was in shambles. Moving slowly and deliberately to the driver's door, he softly exited the car. He was on his bike and headed for home in less than a minute.

The next day, Freddy presented me with a silver metal box. I didn't realize it was a car stereo until I turned it over and saw the knobs and cassette deck.

"Whoa! Where'd you get this?" I roared in surprise.

"I snagged it!" Freddy replied. "I was in a car for almost two hours!"

"No way! Really?"

"There's speakers, too."

He handed me an oil-stained box full of paper rubbish. Under the paper were the four speakers and wiring. We immediately began to install everything in my Corolla while Freddy regaled me with a blow-by-blow description of his adventure in the Maverick. My new stereo fit perfectly where my factory radio had been and the speakers were easily installed in the chintzy cardboard door panels and rear deck. The sound was a quantum leap beyond what I was accustomed to! I was thrilled.

Wherever Freddy, Virge, Jake, and I went in my car, everyone asked me to play their favorite tape or just blast KMET* on that stereo. It was definitely the best thing Freddy had ever stolen, and it was enjoyed by everyone. Nice job, Freddy! It was worth the effort—and the risk! ◼

· CHAPTER 5 ·

ROCKET MANIA

 Freddy and I were always trying to improve the explosives in our arsenal, and the modified "safe and sane" fireworks we changed into rockets were never propelled high enough or fast enough or exploded big enough for our liking. It was only natural that we would take the next logical step to improve our fire power: model rockets turned into exploding missiles. Another innocuous hobby bent to our pyro-maniacal wills!

You could find model rocket engines in most hobby stores, and it seemed Freddy was always pocketing a few with each trip to Hobby City in the Brea Mall. Model rockets could be launched from several hundred to several thousand feet, depending on the class of engine. Our interest didn't lie in making the engines explode (though I'm sure such a thing is possible). We were more interested in lofting and igniting fiery payloads.

In March of 1980, shortly before I moved in with the Filipos, Freddy and I set to work on our first exploding rocket. It was the simplest of all possible designs. A body tube, which normally contained the engine and to which the fins were glued, was completely absent. The body was the engine itself, with the fins fixed directly to the engine. The clay cap in the top of the engine, which was designed to protect a model's parachute, was scratched out (as was done in all following missiles). This modification allowed the hot parachute-ejection charge to ignite combustible payloads on top of it. We glued an empty aluminum Binaca breath spray tube to the top of the engine and capped it with the orange spout from an Elmer's Glue bottle. Inside the Binaca tube was homemade black powder, ground-up magnesium, and BBs. It was quite an odd and amusing thing, as dangerous projectiles go.

We had high hopes for this little marvel. The small engine had the potential to propel the payload two to three hundred feet, and we expected the black powder to explode, sending down a shower of intensely bright burning

The Binaca breath-spray-of-death rocket

magnesium while firing the BB flak in every direction. As you can see by the photo here, we were proud of our creation.

Virge and Freddy and I went to Rose Drive Elementary School the night following the completion of this rocket. Freddy set up the launch pad and rocket on the grassy ball field, attached the micro-clips to the Solar Igniter* in the rocket's engine, and played out the launch wire in the direction of the gate to the bike trail. Without the ceremonious hesitation and last words I came to expect, Freddy pressed the button on the launch controller, and the rocket zipped into the night sky with a sharp hiss and an abundance of smoke. Freddy then darted into the pall of smoke to retrieve the launch pad and wire, and we immediately moved toward the gate, expecting a loud report and a blinding fireball that would bring attention to the scene.

Instead, there was a muffled pop and only the vague sensation that there were BBs and perhaps some rocket parts falling into the tall trees that bordered our escape route. What a miserable disappointment!

One notable (but less devious) rocket endeavor followed shortly after I had taken residence at the Filipos' in April of 1980. Freddy had procured an AstroCam, which was a relatively pricey model rocket with a particular 110 camera[*] built into its nose cone. Finding one in Karl's Hobbies in the Brea Mall, he stripped the cellophane wrapper off of its box right there in the aisle, opened the box, removed all the necessary bagged parts and instructions, and stuffed them under his jacket and into his pants. I witnessed this, and at the time, I was amazed at his speed, dexterity, and sizable balls!

Once Freddy had built this AstroCam, we loaded it with film and wanted to test it. Rather than going to the ballfields at Rose Drive Elementary and getting aerial pictures of an unfamiliar neighborhood, Freddy decided it should be launched from the driveway of his house, hopefully getting a shot of his property. I protested when we discovered there was a wind. I was sure that the rocket would be carried into some far-off yard and get hung up in one of the many tall trees. However, it was Freddy's rocket, and he did with it as he pleased. He took notice of the wind direction and leaned the launch rod on the Porta-Pad* well into it. I couldn't imagine why he was being so foolish.

"SSSSffffissssssh!"

Up went the beautiful AstroCam; 100, 500, 1000 feet on an arching trajectory, taking it over the border into Placentia! Then, red tracking smoke—the rocket seemed a mile away! The plastic 'chute popped out with a jerk and a puff of white smoke, deploying nicely. Down it came from places on high, gently turning, down, down, down. It was getting closer! Would it get hung up in the giant Canary Island pine on the top of Freddy's hill?! No! It landed within ten feet of the launch pad there at the top of the driveway! Would Freddy ever cease to amaze me?

Somehow, Freddy sensed it was risky to try another driveway launch and expect the same results. Also, the rocket wasn't getting a photo of his place. Compensating for the wind took it over strange territory. We then went to Rose Drive Elementary to familiarize ourselves with the camera by taking a few more test shots. Our first launch from the school was done more vertically, and the wind took its due. As the rocket descended, it did so somewhat laterally and crossed Rose Drive. It became neatly suspended by its shroud lines on electrical wires about twenty feet above someone's yard. Of course, we refused to let this beat us. We had the photo from the driveway launch in that thing, and we were going to get it back or be damned.

We approached the woman who resided in the house where our rocket hung, and in some way we were able to convince her we were decent chaps and that we should be allowed to try to retrieve our property. Poles we borrowed weren't long enough to reach it from the ground, so Freddy mounted a cinder block wall separating the houses. Freddy's ascent brought out the next door neighbors who seemed to require an explanation. We told them it was an expensive and valuable aerial photography camera that we were trying to save, and they were suitably impressed and calmed.

This is the box art for the Estes AstroCam as it appeared in 1980.

Eventually, we concluded that nothing we could do would bring down the rocket. It was just too wound around the electrical wire and even whacking it and prying at it would not break the shroud lines that suspended it. It was then that we asked the good woman if we could use her phone.

Immune to the mortal failings of embarrassment and guilt, Freddy called the electric company and gave them the same exaggerations we had fed the neighbors. Within the hour, company pole climbers were indignantly switching off the neighborhood power and poking at the rocket for us. As the lineman on the pole made a particularly dangerous maneuver, a clean-cut and very proper teen in the crowd next door said, "That's just like my AstroCam... They only cost about thirty bucks!"

So much for our impromptu charade. The rocket soon fell into Freddy's hands, and when I asked him what he wanted to do—like say, "thanks"—he just shrugged, blinked, and replied, "Let's go." So, we slipped away before anyone could do a double take.

Who were those masked rocketeers, anyway?

The photo taken during the driveway launch turned out to be part of some unknown yard and a bit of the drainage ditch a block or so behind Freddy's property on the border between Placentia and Yorba Linda. It was hard to pinpoint. The photo taken from the ill-fated Rose Drive Elementary School launch was also a dud, showing just some blurry rooftops and a strip of Rose Drive.

But, back to model rocketry abuse.

Carrying around a bulky plastic launch pad or even just sinking a launch rod into the ground seemed inconvenient where retrieving equipment was concerned—especially when we needed to vacate the area quickly. By this point, we had decided that a rocket bazooka would be a good thing.

Freddy and I put four-inch PVC pipe and fittings together to make a "big bore" gun with an un-screwable blast plate cap on the back and added a wooden handle, which supported a 12V lantern battery. We then installed a trigger button, and the appropriate ignition wiring. I even painted "suburban camouflage" on the thing with my airbrush. Next, we made standard model rockets with body tubes, but with cut-down fins. The idea was that the rockets would rest inside the barrel supported by their fins in the back and a wire leg in the front. You'd press the trigger to set off the Solar Igniter and launch the rocket. It was fully self-contained.

The night Freddy and I first tested the bazooka, we were very mistrustful of it. Freddy was dolled up in a heavy jacket, shop goggles, and a hat to protect himself. When he fired it from the entrance of his driveway up Rose Drive, the rocket corkscrewed wildly for about twenty yards and hit the pavement. The small fins and lack of a guiding launch rod were the cause. We dropped the whole project when we couldn't make fins larger and get the rocket to fit, or get a launch rod to stay straight while suspended horizontally in the barrel.

We then reverted to the old stick-the-rod-in-the-ground approach. Freddy and I had developed quite a few rockets with different payloads and went out with Virge and Jake Faris late one night to test them. The launch site was a vast open field a block away. It sported a few blackened citrus trees, and was otherwise an expanse of grassy moguls. There was a narrow horse trail bordering a wall on the south side of this field, which we used to penetrate to a point reasonably far away from houses. We were able to do all the launching we wanted without fear of capture, if not detection. We even felt confident of escape with Jake along, which is saying something, as the bespectacled fourteen-year-old had a habit of stumbling through the brush and was incapable of fast retreat or wall climbing for being so portly. He had poor eyesight at night, too.

The first rocket featured gasoline-soaked cotton balls resting on wax paper above the engine in the body tube. It whooshed into the heavens several hundred feet and spat out its burning payload. The hot wads looked like giant drunken fireflies making lazy S's as they fell, supported somewhat by their own heat in the cold air.

"People will think it's a UFO invasion!" I smiled.

Somehow, Virge and Freddy weren't convinced.

The next couple of rockets had explosive payloads. Their flights ended with a sudden bang and some trailing embers. They reminded me of a dud signal flare, though I could only imagine what a dud flare might look like, never having seen one.

The loud bangs from these rockets made me nervous. It was only a matter of time before residents reported the explosions, and I felt we had had enough fun for one evening. Luckily, we were out of ammunition, and we returned home without incident.

Rockets were beginning to get old by the time we finished launching from the field with the derelict orange grove. We had to up the ante to keep things exciting—either make the explosions more significant or do something more challenging. We still had some engines, body tubes, and other parts, but it was beyond our means to make the explosive payloads more powerful. We opted to assault the neighborhood with what we had left instead.

In the wee hours of a spring morning, Freddy and Virge and I went to another launching site across Rose Drive from the grove we had used previously. This place was known as "The Field" for as long as I could remember. It was an oft-visited place for lizard hunting and sneak-out campfires during junior high (and, for smoking pot in later, more delinquent years). It was bordered by, and had been diminished by a small tract of homes that was joined to Virge's street in 1976, but as with the bike trail, it was a thoroughfare for many of our activities just the same. It was from this field that we set up to launch what would be our last volley of explosive model rockets.

Finding a soft grassy spot on top of a mound of earth and concrete chunks, Freddy stuck the launch rod into the ground after some unsuccessful probing. The rod was angled to deliver rockets across the drainage ditch separating our neighborhood and an adjacent neighborhood. Homes were less than a hundred yards away in our intended flight path, and things were dead still. Even the crickets knew we were up to no good. Not a chirp.

Glorious and illustrious, this is "The Field" (note caps), the stage of many of our shenanigans and unwholesome nighttime high jinks. This is looking east and slightly north toward the intersection of Bastanchury Road and Rose Drive (1981 photo).

Our rockets split the silence, whooshing into the target area and going off with loud cracks and bursts of glittering embers, sometimes close to the dry shake rooftops. This was alarming! We intended to frighten the residents, not set them on fire!

As Freddy prepared the third rocket, we heard a voice from the dark void on the other side of the drainage ditch.

"Do another one!" taunted a young male voice.

This was quite a surprise and not a pleasant one at that! *We're* the ones to deal out the surprises, not put on a show for some other deranged teen. We halfway wanted to seek out the individual, if only to know where these watchful eyes were, but we were not feeling particularly motivated or industrious. Also (if I may digress), we were to store ill-gotten materials in a metal pipe connected to the drainage ditch much later, and I'm sure the owner of the voice (and his cronies) secretly watched us hide the pilfered goods, only to steal them from us later.

In any case, we felt inept as terrorists, and this marked the end of our model rocket mania. ▪

· CHAPTER 6 ·

I'M BORED. LET'S BUILD A BOMB.

 In 1980, "safe and sane" fireworks were available at stands all over Southern California. The stands magically appeared in shopping center parking lots a week before the 4th of July, covered with their Day-Glo* advertising posters promising all manner of pyrotechnic marvels. Freddy and I always greeted the sight of the long two-by-four and tar paper structures with wide-eyed glee. After all, we had both been pyromaniacs from an early age.

Among our favorite fiery fare were "Piccolo Petes." Piccolo Petes were screaming whistles driven by a small, unimpressive jet of fire. Their appeal was in their obnoxious shriek. We liked "Ground Bloom Flowers," too. These were two-inch paper tubes packed with a fast-burning, non-volatile black powder, bright-burning magnesium, and various other chemicals to vary the color of the display. The jet flame on one end sends the firework spinning at a terrific speed, etching designs on the air that look like lilies or camellias.

When Freddy got his hands on some of Virge's old fireworks that spring, he explained the virtues of the Piccolo Petes. There were two kinds. The first kind—an older and better variety Freddy assured us—could be unwrapped to reveal a thin, bullet-shaped plastic capsule with powder and a fuse inside. Once stripped, these "Petes" could be made into skyrockets with the addition of a broom straw, skinny school cafeteria straw, or bamboo filament as a tail. The second, later kind was designed to prevent such modifications. It contained a small, thick, laminated cardboard tube in place of the plastic capsule. Though these second types made miserable skyrockets for being too heavy, they were a good source of explosive powder. In its packed form, Piccolo Pete powder burned steadily, but when broken up with a few squeezes from pliers, it went off with a terrific bang, reminiscent of an M80.

Ground Bloom Flowers weren't much good broken down, but they could be made to fly if they were sent high enough aloft—again, according to Freddy.

As to what we did with these fireworks, a few stories immediately come to mind, though these stories represent only a fraction of the interesting fireworks and rocketry experiments we performed. These incidents also do well to begin a chronicle of our steady decline into delinquency starting in the spring of 1980 and into the winter of 1981.

My first recollection of messing with Virge's particular batch of fireworks is innocent enough. Freddy's parents were out one Saturday, and Freddy demonstrated the explosive power of a crushed Piccolo Pete by placing it on a sturdy pie pan, standing a foot-long section of four-inch PVC pipe over it, and inserting a perfectly sized wooden finial ball into the tube. The explosive went off with an ear-splitting crack, and the ball practically flew out of sight, hundreds of feet in the air. We did this three or more times and then retreated to the house, just in time to escape Erwin Faris (Virge and Jake's father), who had entered the property through the gate between the Filipo and Faris yards. No doubt he was trying to find out what kind of trouble Freddy and I were getting his boys into. He probably thought we were shooting off guns.

Despite all our pyro-maniacal activities that spring and summer, we somehow continued to elude parents and other (better armed) authorities. On another spring night, when Freddy and Virge's parents were home but otherwise occupied, the three of us went to the bottom of Freddy's grove with a variety of modified fireworks. In addition to Piccolo Pete skyrockets, we had similar projectiles made from the paper cartridges on pinwheels. We would prop these devices on their stiff fuses in the neck of a bottle to launch them.

We started our launches with the pinwheel contraptions. Freddy had insisted that the pinwheel cartridges push a pinwheel around fast enough, so they should be able to lift their own weight when made into a skyrocket. First attempt: The rocket stayed for the duration of its burn in the bottle. Attempt number two: The rocket made it out of the bottle, but swaggered menacingly in the air a few feet above the ground and hit the ground spent.

We then turned to our Piccolo Pete rockets. The first one whisked into the air with an abbreviated shriek and a bang. It never even cleared the pines bordering the bottom of Freddy's hill. It obviously had a good bit of loose powder in it. The next one flew off south down Rose Drive with an amazingly long burn, and I feared it would strike a car for traveling so low and so parallel to the street.

We next launched a final pinwheel rocket. Much to our surprise, the thing crept into the air, higher and higher, arching over Rose Drive. I was sure it had landed harmlessly in the big yard across the street, but Virge frantically insisted it had fallen on the roof of a house there. We waited momentarily for any ensuing fire, and seeing none, went back to business.

About five minutes later, a man popped into the grove. I saw him first and thought it was only prudent to lunge into nearby bushes to hide. Unfortunately, Freddy and Virge were preoccupied in the open on the driveway and were taken completely by surprise. The man was the owner of the house across the street, and he politely asked that we not shoot off any more skyrockets. The pinwheel skyrocket had indeed landed on his roof. Discovered, and almost out of ammo, we called it quits for the evening—but only after I received a scolding for hiding. "He totally saw you!" Virge told me in a shrill tone.

By the time summer arrived, simple bottle rockets became stale child's play. We were now at a point where things needed to be notched up a bit to keep things interesting. In the area of fireworks, Freddy and I were always baking plots to create bigger and better explosives. Having exhausted the potential of standard fireworks and exploding model rockets, we turned to the design of ingenious bombs.

One thing we were sure of: our little safe and sane explosives weren't fiery enough; gasoline needed to play a part in the next experiment, ideally atomized gasoline, and lots of it. The charge had to blow the gas into the air and ignite it. After some serious thought and a few sketches, Freddy and I set to work on "The Bomb."

Virge, as usual, could only offer a smile of delight and his assistance in rigging the thing at an appropriate detonation time and place.

The Bomb was a huge mayonnaise jar filled with gasoline. Suspended inside it, submerged in the gas, was a baby food jar filled with loose Piccolo Pete powder. A metal tube ran through the lid of the baby food jar, and up through the mayonnaise lid, with epoxy sealing all the seams. Through this tube, Freddy ran two wires connected to a Solar Igniter, typically used to light model rocket engines. One wire connected to one of two batteries in a homemade receptacle, and the other was attached to the minute hand of a cheap plastic alarm clock. With the clock wound and running, the minute hand wire would eventually rotate into connection with the batteries to make an electrical circuit. The flow of electricity would light the igniter, set off the powder, and hopefully atomize and ignite the gasoline.

Once our little marvel was complete, Virge and Freddy and I made arrangements to suspend The Bomb from a light pole on tennis courts at Rose Drive Elementary School—easily seen from the huge Canary Island pine on top of Freddy's hill. We figured if we did this late at night when the court's lights were off, we could rig the explosive without being noticed and go back to Freddy's hill and watch at a safe distance.

Of course, we only gave a little thought to the safety of nearby houses. On the designated night, we would hang the explosive on the light farthest from structures. To do more was asking us to defuse substantial excitement over what was intended to be just an experiment.

Rose Drive Elementary was the scene of many of our exploits over the years, ranging from midnight rocket launches and nighttime kite flying to smoke-outs and all-out fireworks wars with other neighborhood teens. The night we rigged The Bomb, the entire place was dark, and though dogs were doing their full loud bit to protect the neighborhood, we were undisturbed and presumably unnoticed.

We threw some line over the light, set The Bomb's clock for fifteen minutes, and hoisted it to about twenty feet above the tennis courts before tying it off. We then hurried back to Freddy's house veiled in the dark shadows of the bike trail—our favorite artery for evil deeds, which for all practical purposes emptied onto the street in front of Freddy's property.

We then scaled the Canary Island pine, which was a simple matter as the branches took the form of a spiraling ladder. From the top of this tree, Freddy and I had earlier staged an assault on surrounding homes with Wrist Rocket slingshots—only to have two enormous, surly fellows show up at the front door a week later asking, "Do you have green marbles?"

That night, the tree was the perfect platform from which to watch our experiment. We had a clear, uninterrupted view of the tennis court lights poking up above the rooftops two blocks away. I could even make out the light-colored speck that was The Bomb.

The three of us sat in that tree for what seemed like an hour. Freddy's watch and the clock on The Bomb weren't remotely close to being synchronized, if such were even possible.

"It should've gone off by now," Freddy finally said.

An additional minute passed, and I declared it a "dud."

Suddenly, the sky split with a flash of light and then a startling report. The explosion didn't ignite the gas, but the sheer power of the charge was impressive enough. Smoke and gasoline vapor hung in a pall over the tennis courts, which lasted for quite some time.

The next day at Volt, where I worked as a display ad artist for the Yellow Pages, I asked a co-worker named Mary if she had heard anything unusual the night before. I knew Mary lived in Placentia, not more than a half mile as-the-crow-flies from our little firecracker. She admitted that a blast had awakened her and said it sounded like a shotgun going off. This bomb of ours had impacted a lot of people over a wide area, and I have to admit to being rather pleased, despite the lack of a mushroom fireball. Confusing (and presumably frightening) such a large number of people had a certain feeling of power connected with it.

I left work that afternoon to join Freddy and Virge on an inspection of the damage. The light cover—a full three feet of some thick, pebbled Plexiglas material—had been dispersed over a wide area in the form of small shards and pellets. The metal cowling was bent and scorched, and the bulbs themselves were completely gone. As we left across the playing field, we found bits of the plastic alarm clock and a battery, which were almost fifty yards from the light. Just goes to show what a little Piccolo Pete powder can do!

Dreams of mushrooming red balls of fire eventually passed after the event at Rose Drive Elementary. Other forms of skulduggery demanded our attention. By the time the winter of 1981 rolled in, so much wanton crime had gone on that I refrained from outings with Virge and Freddy for fear of being caught, identified, and prosecuted. I had been popped for shoplifting in November, and my fingerprints were recorded at the police station when I was taken into custody. Foolishly enough, I later left fingerprints at the scene of a burglary at Yorba Linda Middle School (Jake Faris' school). I could feel the hot breath of the law heaving at my collar. So, Freddy and Virge became a dastardly duo of detonations.

Despite our (albeit limited) success with The Bomb at Rose Drive Elementary School, Virge and Freddy did endeavor to test one new form of bomb. I witnessed its construction, but I'll have to trust their account of its detonation. I refused to be there. And, I have no reason to doubt their report, as it was consistent with many of our experiences. Said bomb was a gallon Gallo* glass wine jug filled with gasoline. A standard test tube, full of loose Piccolo Pete powder, was neatly suspended in the neck of the wine bottle by its rim. A long piece of cannon fuse was inserted into the powder. Voilà!—Instant death and destruction—what more could a teenage boy desire? (Well, maybe a girlfriend. A girlfriend who likes explosives.)

The bike trail, formally known as the "El Cajon Trail," was often critical to our exploits, as it offered a dimly lit escape route opening onto many streets and pedestrian accesses but forbidden to cars. We always felt confident that we could go where vehicles couldn't and that we could baffle the cops by mixing up our routes at a whim, launching into any of a number of bordering neighborhoods. Admittedly, this knowledge made Virge and Freddy as confident as ever. They snuck out in the wee hours of one night with the new explosive and pedaled off on their ten-speeds to a quiet cul-de-sac several blocks away that terminated at, and had an outlet to the bike trail.

There was not a soul to be seen (or so they thought), and they placed the bomb in the middle of the cul-de-sac, lit the fuse, and went back to the trail to watch from their bikes. As the cherry on the long fuse crept to the powder, Virge noticed a man in a bathrobe, smoking a cigarette, watching everything somewhat dispassionately from the darkened entry of his house. The headlights of a car approaching the area could also be seen about a block away. Then, "BOOM!" A huge red-orange mushroom of fire rose over the street, illuminating it in an eerie glow. Streams of fire swept across the entire street, up both curbs, and across the grass parkways. The man who stood in his entry darted for his garden hose. The car came to an abrupt stop. Virge and Freddy split—in awe. Well done, boys. ∎

Here's a digital recreation of Freddy and Virge's Gallo fire bomb, based on their eyewitness reports. The actual cul-de-sac is shown (present day).
There's a lot of potential energy in one gallon of gasoline!

· CHAPTER 7 ·

THE FIREWORKS HEIST AND MORE

 By now, Dear Reader, you know that Virge, Freddy, and I were heavily into the fireworks thing for a year or so. As our resources were depleted in various neighborhood-rocking exploits, we made plans to knock over a firework stand. That's right! It seemed the only logical route to obtain all the raw materials for mayhem we would ever need.

When June of 1980 rolled around, and the various organizations began to erect their plywood fire-brothels, we cased a particular outlet on a dirt lot perhaps three-quarters of a mile down Rose Drive. It looked to be a dark, isolated spot at night, and our plan involved removing the door lock's hasp while the stand was still empty. We'd then remove the pin in the hasp in Freddy's garage by severing the head of the pin, and then glue the pin and head back together in the hinge of the hasp so it would work temporarily. We would then reinstall the whole thing before anyone was the wiser. With such a prearranged state of affairs, we could separate the locked hasp with just a little force against the glue and get into the stand on a night when it was fully stocked.

The nighttime removal of the hasp, its modification, and re-installation all went as planned, and a few days later I found myself driving Freddy and Virge to the scene of the crime in my tin-can '72 Toyota Corolla at 3:00 a.m. We parked in an unlit lot behind the Placentia-Linda Hospital, gathered up an array of duffel bags, flashlights, and homemade nightsticks, and walked the half block or so to the fireworks stand using a dark and little-used lane that lay behind it.

At this point, I was having second thoughts about the whole affair. Not so much because I would be depriving some upstanding community organization of cash for their program encouraging Chinese prostitutes to drink more responsibly (or whatever), but because I might have to defend myself from some charging fireworks proprietor with a whittled piece of 2x2! It had been of some concern to me that someone might be stationed at, or even sleeping *in* the stand. Even though Virge and Freddy had helped man fireworks stands as Boy Scouts when they were larvae, and they insisted that this was highly unlikely, the potential for someone getting badly hurt was still pretty sizable. I'm not violent by nature, and in any other circumstance, I might have laid down arms and retreated when discovered. Unfortunately, there were peer pressures to defend ourselves and each other, and nervous tension was running high. I was in the uncomfortable position of possibly clobbering some poor chap, or even his poodle-toting, two-tons-of-fun Mamacita.

Once we arrived at the stand, we found a darkened motor home guarding. Luckily, it was especially dark that night, and no one seemed to be up and about. Before getting to the task, we began to argue in hushed tones.

"Let's go!" I said.

"No. You stay here and watch," Virge replied. "Freddy and I are going up!"

"No! I want to go!" I insisted. "Why do you and Freddy get to go, and I don't?"

"You need to watch the trailer!" was Virge's response.

"No!" I said.

I was adamant. Who made flipper-footed Virge the commander of this little expedition? Then Freddy chimed in to support Virge.

"Just stay here and watch!"

Before I knew it, they were making for the stand, and I was left to deal with anyone exiting the motor home. I experienced an odd mixture of anger and anxiety, made all the more difficult by a feeling that Virge and Freddy were in cahoots over something else. But, someone needed to protect whoever did the actual entry. They'd be wrestling with opening the door and would be behind a small enclosed "wing" on the stand with all attention fixed on the lock. Unguarded, intruders could easily be surprised.

The noises Freddy and Virge created while trying to release the hasp were distressing! There were popping and prying sounds louder than any alarm! Or so it seemed. Though they successfully released the pin, the door opened out, and the hasp had to be bent so the door would clear it. The bulky padlock in place prevented the hasp from being bent much, but somehow they were able to mangle the hasp enough. We hadn't planned on the inordinate amount of time it took to do this.

The door freed, my two fellow merry pyromaniacs had unfettered access and they began pillaging the stand. Despite the noise created getting in, there had not been one sign of life from the motor home, which was thirty feet behind the structure. It was cold enough that the three of us were wearing jackets, and chances were all the windows on the motor home were shut tight.

I concluded that our chance of discovery was slim at this point and that I should take part in the looting. Virge and Freddy were quickly and carefully stuffing the duffel bags with the choicest individual items when I came to the door. They were both startled when I popped in, thinking they'd been nabbed.

Virge voiced his reluctance to let me stuff bags when I could be watching for the proprietors. Freddy, who was smiling gleefully and seemed glad of my appearance, proudly hoisted a heavy steel cylinder.

"Look what I found!"

"What is it?" I whispered, not recognizing the shape.

"A fire extinguisher!" he responded with a huge, shit-eating grin.

I wasn't realizing the potential of such an item at the time, and wondered why Freddy wanted to lug it. I then began looking around the confines of the stand's interior using my dim flashlight beam. The place was packed from stem to stern with loose and boxed fireworks. It was hard to move around because of it all. It was a dream come true!

"Whoa! Look at all this stuff!" I whispered in awe. "Get a Block Party! Did you get a Block Party?!"

Having the Block Party assortment was a dream each one of us had had at one time or another. It was the most extensive and expensive boxed assortment—that big impressive thing we begged for every year, only to get that particular sneer from our parents. Freddy found the closest thing to the Block Party, the Forty Niner Assortment, and stuffed it into his canvas bag. Piccolo Petes and Ground Bloom Flowers were also at the top of our list, and these went into our sacks by the handful. I don't believe we left a single one.

After ten minutes or so, our many bags, including a huge military duffel, were packed to capacity. We agreed that we had gotten as much as we needed (and more) and began to leave.

It still amazes me that no one in an adjacent condominium complex saw us march down the lane laden like Tolkienian* dwarves coming back from a mining expedition. We were carrying loads that anyone else would have done in two trips! When we packed my car's trunk, we could hardly get everything to fit, and I was anxious to be done with the whole affair. We were vulnerable while lingering over the packing.

"What was that?" I asked in heart-pounding reaction to some far-off traffic sound.

"It's nothing!" Virge said confidently, patronizing me.

"No! Listen!" I insisted. "It sounds like a car is coming through the parking lot!"

The little hospital clinic building was between us and its parking lot proper, and I feared we would be surprised by some squad car turning the corner of the building on its nightly rounds. But, artless as he was, Virge was right (and I hated when he was right!). It was nothing. My adrenaline was kicking in with every little sound.

After Freddy made one more quick trip back to the stand for the fire extinguisher, which I protested, we somehow managed to pack in our take and returned home without complications.

I drove past the fireworks stand on my way to work later that morning. There was not one, but two squad cars parked there! It was only then that the full weight of what we had done struck me. Of course, I became quite nervous and somewhat guilt-ridden. I prayed that no one had seen us leave the scene or had identified my car. Later that day, when Freddy and Virge were told of what I saw, they responded with indifference. We all knew that the police would be called to the scene, but for me, actually seeing it made the reality particularly clear.

The fireworks stash stayed in my trunk until a time when I worried it would ignite in the summer's heat. We moved everything into one of what are best described as "utility closets" at the back of the Filipo property that had been given to Freddy and me by his parents. But as it goes, we feared it would eventually be stumbled upon by Arnie. Its ultimate resting place was in an industrial-size, cylindrical cardboard "ice-cream" container, which was hidden among others like it on a deep, overhanging shelf in the back of Freddy's garage. The shelf was the family's black hole—a place where things were stored and never looked at again. The hiding place was Freddy's final decision, and if he was happy with it, I was too.

AFTER THE HEIST

Now that we had an enormous larder of combustibles, we began new experiments. Freddy was the first to suggest a detonation of a large amount of loose Piccolo Pete powder. He found a sturdy plastic bottle with a screw-on lid about the size of a 7.5oz mini soda can and set to the task of extracting the powder. The bottle was eventually filled, and a piece of cannon fuse was inserted through a small hole drilled in the lid, which was screwed down extra tight.

Our target was to be car glass, and we knew that we couldn't detonate our new toy too close to home. It was a situation and an explosive that would be too unpredictable. We set off on our ten-speeds down the bike trail in the dark morning hours of a summer Sunday, penetrating more deeply into the center of Yorba Linda than we were accustomed.

After pedaling two miles, we came upon a pedestrian accessway that linked Wisteria Drive and the bike trail. The whole Wisteria cul-de-sac was visible from the trail and there was an abundance of vehicles. Freddy announced that he was going to duct-tape the Piccolo Pete bomb to the rear windshield of a GMC Jimmy* parked in the driveway of a home three houses in. I protested. I thought Freddy would be plain to see (and easily described) because the street had abundant artificial light. Freddy didn't care. He quickly entered the cul-de-sac and began taping the bomb to the Jimmy's back window with some difficulty. The duct tape wasn't sticking. He kept adding strip after strip. An excessive amount of time passed, and Virge and I worried aloud that Freddy was taking a big gamble. Finally, Freddy lit the fuse and ran back to our position on the bike trail.

"CRAAACK!" The device went off with an eardrum-numbing discharge and an enormous pall of gray smoke.

We stretched our necks for precious seconds, waiting for the smoke to clear. What was the damage?! Zip. Zilch. Nil. Nada. We could see the shape of the former, now pulverized plastic bottle neatly outlined by a star burst of ash on the unscathed tinted window.

"Nothing!" burped Virge.

"Shit!" I said. "Let's get out of here! C'mon! Quick!"

Off we went down the trail toward home.

After a mile, we found ourselves on an especially dark stretch of the bike trail, halfway between Valley View and Prospect Avenues. Freddy slowed down and eased over to the pathway's edge where homes could be seen at the bottom of a steep bank.

"What are you doing?" I asked.

"Let's throw some Ground Bloom Flowers into that pool!" Freddy recommended.

Virge and I were curious where this would lead, and Freddy was quick to launch a couple of the spinning devices through a tree line and into a built-in pool. They hissed and spit and bubbled while emitting an eerie light. No reaction from the homeowners. Just as Freddy was throwing a third one, Virge straightened up suddenly.

"Cops! The cops are coming!"

Sure enough, we could see a spotlight scanning back and forth behind a rise about two blocks up the trail where we had just been. The police were unusually quick to respond to the explosion on Wisteria Drive.

We took off in a panic at top speed. After a block-long stretch of trail, when we reached the accessway to Santa Fe Street, I called to my furiously pedaling comrades.

"Here! Santa Fe! This way!"

I was quickly dismissed as Freddy and Virge continued straight down the trail. I was sure that their route, though direct, was the same route the squad car was taking. Fuck those morons. I turned onto Santa Fe Street. The cops' vehicle would never be able to squeeze through the narrow pedestrian access.

Once on Santa Fe, I heard a vehicle approaching. I immediately ditched my bike into a juniper hedge behind a low wall on the corner of Santa Fe and Aries Drive. It was a civilian, and they passed by without slowing down. I then navigated the unfamiliar neighborhood with just a vague sense of which way was south and which way was west and eventually found myself on Rose Drive, over half a mile south of the Filipos' house. I waited another ten minutes and struck out onto Rose Drive where I could easily be seen. Traffic was almost non-existent, but it was the longest half mile of my life! I arrived home without further incident, still sweating bullets. Virge and

Freddy also made it back safely, which was much to my amazement. They both got a piece of my mind, just the same.

Despite experimenting with a fair number of the goodies we pilfered from the fireworks stand, we never used a fraction of the number we took, and I don't precisely recall the ultimate fate of everything. I have a notion that Freddy discarded the whole lot at some point, not wishing to tempt fate.

On the next page is the typed inventory Freddy made of our booty. Yes, the final tabulation is right. A retail value of almost $1,100 in 1980 dollars. With a cumulative rate of inflation, this would be worth $3,325 today. ■

Fireworks Inventory

Item	Description	Quantity	Price
Ground Bloom Flowers	Pkg. of 4	358	358.00
Piccolo Petes		329	115.15
Sparklers	8 #10	131	85.15
" "	6 Pkgs.6 #8	3	5.94
Calif. Candles	Jumbo	15	22.50
" "	Lagre	10	10.00
" " .	Small	9	6.75
" "	Mystery	6	6.00
Cosmos	Cone	3	5.25
Queen Of Hearts	Cone	2	3.50
Jumbo Carnival	Cone	4	7.00
Giant Silver Screemer	Cone	18	31.50
Giant Brilliant	Cone	9	13.50
Giant Bulls Eye	Cone	9	13.50
King Kong	Base Fountain	8	14.00
Cascade	#3 Base Fountain	9	15.75
Yanky Doodle Salute	Base Fountain	3	5.25
Star Spangled Salute	Base Fountain	3	5.25
Sky Shower	Base fountain	4	7.00
Mystery Cone		6	6.00
Tuneful Towers	BAse Fountain	12	21.00
Tower Of Jewles	Base Fountain	6	7.50
Gemini V	Base Fountain	2	3.50
Piery Echo	Base Fountain	2	5.00
Columbia	Base Fountain	1	2.50
Screaming Meemie	Base Fountain	1	2.50
Musical Duet	Base Fountain	2	5.00
Grand Finale	Base Fountain	6	7.50
Vesuvius	Base Fountain	12	9.00
Pinwheels	Moon and Star2 Dr.	24	18.00
"	Moon and Star 3 Dr.	15	15.00
" .	Rainbow Triangles	25	25.00
"	Jumbo	3	18.00
"	Medium	3	15.00
Small Box Fire		35	8.75
Silver Shower	#1	33	4.95
Friendship	Small Fountain	24	12.00
Witches Caldron		18	4.20
Colorful Flare		72	7.20
Smoke Balls	Pkg. of 6	10	10.00
Daylight Smoke		14	7.00
Multi Color Smoke	Pkg. of 2	36	18.00
Party Poppers		48	4.80
Bang Site	Tubes	10	10.00
Bang Site Canons		4	60.00
Forty Niner	Assortment	1	50.00

Total

1088.69

· CHAPTER 8 ·

SPLASHIN'

 It had always bemused me to think that Yorba Linda had no high school of its own and had to bus its students to campuses in Fullerton. Virge (a senior) and Freddy (a junior) were students at Troy High School in 1980, and like any high school, Troy had its share of miscreants from which to learn. Thanks to the escapades of a few unwashed, unnamed leaping gnomes who enjoyed hosing down the locals, Freddy learned that there were water-filled fire extinguishers that could be refilled with a garden hose and then charged with air pressure at the local gas station. To Freddy, this activity sounded like an exciting diversion, and he remained on the lookout for such a device until we procured one when knocking over the fireworks stand. Not to be out-dicked by the fairy-folk mentioned above, July of 1980 saw our very own campaign to wet the public.

Virge and Freddy and I first tested the extinguisher on the driveway at Freddy's house while his parents were out. It was big, heavy, and cumbersome when filled with water, and it was hard to imagine anyone whisking it off to a fire! Freddy pressed the tab on the nozzle, and a thick, powerful stream shot out to a distance of perhaps fifty feet. We were impressed and anxious to try it on unsuspecting victims! However, with all our "testing," the charge was soon depleted.

We then found ourselves recharging the extinguisher at the Arco station on the corner of Imperial Highway and Rose Drive. It was a bright, hot day, and the station was bustling. While Freddy hooked up the air hose, and Virge and I stood by, we received our share of knowing looks, as well as squeals of encouragement from other youth. Virge would smile and nod, acknowledging our intent. But, now that we were celebrities, we figured it would be best to use the extinguisher in a town other than Yorba Linda. Also, the fireworks heist was still fresh. Should we get pulled over on a traffic stop, the cops could confiscate it, match the serial number on it, and then where would we be? No. Yorba Linda would never do.

Rod Stewart had a rather insipid tune on the radio at the time entitled *Passion*. However, the refrain of the word "passion" was catchy. Someone's car stereo at the Arco station played this song, and Freddy's head bobbed up and down to the music.

"Splashin'!" He sang, rather pleased with his parody.

He pointed to the extinguisher.

"Hey, Virge!… 'Splashin'!'"

We were only politely amused, but the name stuck to our hobby about as much as did the term "fire-extinguishing."

Our first night out with our new toy was not the orgy of "blasting" we hoped it would be. We had to scour large portions of Brea and Fullerton and found only three suitable targets. We were in my Corolla, which was the only vehicle to which any of us had any ready access. I was driving, of course. Virge sat in the front passenger seat with a tape recorder and his 35mm camera, Virge's fourteen-year-old brother, Jake, sat behind Virge with the extinguisher between his legs, and Freddy sat next to Jake in the back. We had no intention of squirting folks frequently, as we had a consensus that this would eventually bring the law down on us. We also wanted to preserve what few exploits we expected to have, and the recorder and camera facilitated this.

We told the parents that we were going to a movie in Brea and that we'd be out late. We started splashin' around midnight. Finding a suitable victim was not as easy as we had hoped, and seemed to take an inordinate amount of time. Eventually, we found ourselves traveling east on Imperial Highway where we saw a seventeen- or eighteen-year-old stoner trudging along the sidewalk between Puente and Jasmine streets. We pulled over and engaged the fellow in conversation. Unknown to this person, Virge had the recorder running and taped our short, but striking discourse on the topics of a local party, pot, booze, and various other unwholesome things. The guy wanted a ride and would talk a bit to get one, though he never asked for one outright. We were all chuckling to ourselves, particularly Virge, and I'm sure this made the guy apprehensive. We also gave no appearance that we had any room for a fifth passenger, or had any intention of giving him a lift, even though Virge hinted we were going in his direction.

Figure 1: Whip it! Whip it good!

Figure 2: The fucked and the motherfuckers

I soon tired of the exchange and said to the dude, "We want to get your picture!" hoping this would get the guy away from his position leaning on Virge's door and back onto the sidewalk. After some good-humored deliberation, the youth stood back just right. Virge raised the camera, and with the word "NOW!" Jake zapped the poor bastard (fig. 1). The camera flash went off as our first victim whipped away madly and fell headfirst into a planter at the back of the sidewalk. In another wild twisting movement, he fell away from the planter with a snap of his arm, hurling a wood chip. We were soon out of range of any more projectiles.

"Did you see that?!" Virge laughed. "That guy freaked out!"

"Yeah! That was great!" I said.

"That was the biggest freak[out] I've ever seen!" Freddy chimed in.

More fruitless driving followed, so we began to head home, hoping something would pop up en route. We were in Fullerton by the time we found our next target. We found this victim on the corner of Placentia Avenue and Yorba Linda Boulevard. He looked to be a sixteen- or seventeen-year-old, and he was lingering on a gas station lot there. When we pulled over, he eagerly approached the car. He was sure we were going to give him a lift. Instead, he got a heavy-duty "splash" (fig. 2). His imaginative cry of "motherfucker!" was duly noted.

Farther down Yorba Linda Boulevard we found another gentleman who was toting a bota bag. We slowed and ventured a squirt, but this individual was out of range (The photo taken was blocked by something in the car as well. I can only blame haste).

By this time it was 2:00 a.m. or so, and we continued toward home. The consensus was that we were experiencing some pretty lean pickin's. It was a grand first night out though, even if the driving and searching were a bit time consuming.

Despite the scarcity of suitable targets our first night out, we undertook a second foray near Fullerton Junior College no more than a week later. After cruising past a group of Latino types in a mini-mart parking lot who we suspected were up to no good, we spied two others walking down a narrow lane lined with old homes. These would be our first victims of the night.

I drove past the men, and to get them on the extinguisher side of my car, I made a left onto another street, turned around, and waited at a stop sign there. I pulled out when the men were at mid-block, cruised up to them, and stopped. Virge asked some insipid question of them, which drew them closer to the car. Jake then unleashed a torrent of water (fig. 3). One of the two men doesn't appear in the photo, but both were drenched. The look on the face of the man in the picture became synonymous with our squirt-ventures. The smile-like grimace on his face gave us intermittent giggles the rest of the evening.

It wasn't too much farther before we managed to hose a fellow on the sidewalk in a "drive-by" hosing (fig. 4). Next, we cruised down the small residential streets looking for isolated victims. We saw no one and began complaining that we'd have to go home without another score. As I approached an intersection where an apartment complex faced us, we saw another Chicano guy exiting the complex's parking area on foot. I pulled over next to this young man, who wanted to respond to Virge's need for directions, but spoke little or no English. Jake doused him in response to our impatient urgings of "NOW!" and the man turned tail into the dark parking stalls from which he came (fig. 5).

With this success, we went to Cal State Fullerton, hoping to find college-student types loitering in drunken states on the corners there. After stopping to allow Jake and Freddy to change positions, we were able to do a long-range blast on a man outside of Denny's restaurant on Chapman Avenue (fig. 6).

Not far from the Denny's spritz, Virge asked directions of another man, who approached the car. This guy was immediately blasted, but rather than fleeing, he ran a few yards and then turned to charge my car. He hurled a towel at us, slapped the trunk of my car, and let us have a few choice words. It's not surprising that we got no photo of this. It happened *very* quickly, and the reaction we evoked was startling. I was having second thoughts about this new amusement of ours. I began to imagine what would happen if such a macho guy were able to get into his bitchin' Camaro, chase us down and do us some kind of damage.

This final splash capped the evening and did a lot to dampen my enthusiasm for our new sport. However, once our photos were developed, that of the service-station chap and the others became prized possessions, always good to induce a laugh or two.

Figure 3: Grimace for the camera!

Figure 4: Hope this cleans your whites!

The next night out with the fire extinguisher came a few days later. We became bold enough to use it near home in Yorba Linda, and Freddy, Virge, and I went into a nearby neighborhood at the modest hour of 8:00 p.m. We were in my Corolla again, this time with Freddy sitting behind me with the extinguisher. Virge sat in the front passenger seat, per usual.

After some half-hearted searching, we entered a residential street and approached a toy-cluttered yard full of kids there. I stopped, and Virge leaned over me, addressing a boy who was straddling a bicycle on the driveway.

Figure 5: ¡Más rápido, Jorge! ¡Más rápido!

"Do you know how to get to Skaggs?"* Virge asked, which was ridiculous, as the sign for this particular drug store could be seen shining only two blocks away.

"Uh, yeah... You see that..." The child started.

Before he could finish, Freddy let the stream fly. The kids scattered with sharp cries as the cold water swept across them.

I felt squirting little kids was really cheap. Also, my thoughts about the enraged fellow with the towel came back to haunt me, and I imagined a posse

Figure 6: Caught in a game of pocket pool!

of angry parents striking out to find us in the family station wagons. We had no other success on this particular outing, and this would be the last I would attend.

Like all of our other projects, splashin' had to be taken up a notch by Freddy. Into the next tank of water, Freddy mixed red tempera paint we had gotten from a breaking-and-entering raid on a supply room at Rose Drive Elementary School. He then went out with someone he knew from school who had a car and hosed a few more youngsters. He showed me a photo of some child's backside as they ran from the pink stream. It was only mildly amusing to think what mark this may have made on the kid's clothing (what about the mark on their consciousness?). Somehow, this had gotten a bit too sociopathic for my liking. I'm glad the whole practice quickly faded away, and, in a sense, we can thank Freddy's dad for this.

Arnie Filipo eventually came upon the extinguisher. When he asked Freddy where he got it, Freddy lied and said he had bought it from a friend to protect the utility shed we used to store stray articles.

"These need to be registered with the fire department!" Arnie demanded.

Of course, we couldn't do such a thing—it belonged to the fireworks stand we had knocked over. But, Arnie being Arnie, he wasn't about to let us keep the extinguisher unless we had it recorded. I even have a recollection of him offering to take it down to the fire station for us—much to our dismay! After we denied him the pleasure, the elder Filipo would occasionally bring up the subject of registering the thing. The extinguisher was then hidden, hoping it was a case of "out of sight, out of mind." Unfortunately, Arnie had tenacity if not brains. Freddy eventually had to dispose of the extinguisher altogether. So much for Splashin'. ◾

· CHAPTER 9 ·

BE CRUEL TO YOUR SCHOOL

 Freddy and I were always up for a new challenge. And, we always had some kind of building project going on. At one point we built a six-foot-tall conyne kite,* which we used to drop streams of aluminum cans onto the neighborhood. We even lifted a wooden chair with it. Yes, we were always in need of materials, especially free materials.

It was a summer day when Freddy came upon the notion that we should walk down to Rose Drive Elementary School and see if we could force entry into a utility room there. After dark, and still at an early hour, we traipsed the two blocks to the school using the bike trail. The trail had a gate between it and the school's ballfields, which was usually locked when classes weren't in session. It was always easy to scale.

Freddy led me to an unlit building on the east side of the small campus and showed me the door to the storage room in question. It had a sturdy steel plate concealing the lock mechanism, but just barely concealing it. There was enough space between the steel plate and the door frame that Freddy could probe and pry with a stiff credit card he had "borrowed" from his mother's purse. He discovered that it wasn't a deadbolt. It was a simple latch bolt, a stupid design from a security standpoint!

"This isn't going to work," I said.

This was taking a lot longer than my patience allowed.

"No. I can get it!" Freddy insisted.

Sure enough, the plastic card was enough to slide back the latch a tiny bit and the door was open.

We hadn't thought to bring flashlights, so the door was swung wide to allow what little ambient light there was to penetrate into the darkness. The utility room was bigger than I expected. About two-hundred square feet. There was so much junk stored there that we had trouble navigating through it.

There were glass windows and a door at the far end of the room, which was an access to the classrooms. Naturally, Freddy tested the door. It was locked.

Floor-to-ceiling metal shelves lined two walls. There were boxes and industrial-size buckets crammed onto every square inch. Mops, wheeled cleaning buckets, "wet floor" signs, traffic cones, and janitorial materials covered the floor.

"Look at all of this crap!" I said, doubtful that there was anything useful to us.

"What are these?" Freddy asked, wrangling a giant, pristine sheet of cardboard from behind a tower of boxes. "It's a voting booth!"

"What good is a voting booth?" I inquired.

"I dunno. It's a lot of good cardboard. We can make something with it."

"Okay. But I'm not carrying it back… Where will we hide something that big?"

This is the view of Rose Drive Elementary School from its back gate at the bike trail sometime in the 80s. The arrow points to a recess between classrooms where we entered through a utility room door.

"There's plenty of room in the utility shed at home."

Two voting booths were placed by the door to the outside. We began rummaging through the boxes on the shelves next to the door and came upon something that looked familiar. Tempera paint. Dozens of boxed plastic bottles of it.

"I think I can use some of this paint for an art project," I announced.

"Let's paint the room!" Freddy hooted in response.

The tempera paint was thick, almost a paste. With a lot of shaking and a little experimentation, we found that if we squeezed the bottles while giving them a hard over-hand jerk the paint could be thrown in globs and long ribbons. The walls and shelves were thoroughly doused with red and green and blue pigments, while we giggled like school girls. It stuck to everything like glue.

Freddy and I then left with the voting booths and a few bottles of paint.

Why we weren't seen and reported while carrying the conspicuous cardboard booty will always remain a mystery. Obviously, there were no motion sensors in the utility room. But, what about the classrooms?

Of course, Virge was eager to learn all of the details of our little quest. Though our take had been paltry, he wanted to go back to the school to see if the interior door to the classrooms could be cracked.

The three of us went back about a week later. Freddy brought a flathead screwdriver this time and the utility room door was opened in less than a minute. Someone had scrubbed off the paint on the walls and the materials on the shelves. Tempera is a water-based paint, but the pigment still left obvious stains on the walls. Most of the junk that had been stored on the floor had been moved around, too. It was an easier matter to get to the back of the room where the glass door to the classrooms stood. To our astonishment, this door was unlocked. The janitor had been incredibly careless, especially after the earlier break-in.

We wandered into the first classroom. Windows lined three of the walls. There was enough artificial light coming in from outside that we didn't require flashlights. I began to rummage through the teacher's desk.

"So, Virge, is this one of the classrooms you had as a kid?"

"No," he said, standing in the middle of the classroom looking rather bored.

I think he was ashamed that we were essentially stealing from kids. I have to admit that I felt this whole undertaking was pretty cheap. But, I still got a kick out of burglarizing a place. Anyplace. It was exciting.

"We should make this quick. There might be motion sensors in these classrooms. Is there anything you wanted?"

"Nah. There's nothing here I want."

He hadn't even looked.

I found some drawing tools in the teacher's desk—pencils, crayons, rulers, pads, triangles, and a protractor. I grabbed them and stuffed them into a pillowcase I had brought with me.

We moved to another classroom at the other end of the building. Freddy was going through the tall cabinets there.

I had been brewing a bowel movement for quite a while, and its delivery time had arrived. This wasn't the first escapade where I had the nagging urge to shit. Maybe it was the fresh night air or general atmosphere of excitement. I had dropped a massive load in a jacuzzi-style bathtub in the unfinished houses across from Freddy's place recently. We often passed through the construction site on our way to the bike trail. In any case, history was about to repeat itself.

"I have to take a dump!" I announced.

"Use the bathrooms!" Virge told me in disgust.

I tottered into the hallway to where I had seen the boys' and girls' restrooms. Locked! Both of them! Jesus, the people who secured this place at night sure had their priorities fucked up! I went back into the classroom where Freddy was still scouring the cabinets. I was going to have to be creative. There was a large window and the usual stainless steel sink in the corner—a loaded paper towel dispenser, too. This would do.

"What are you doing?!" Freddy yapped as I dropped my drawers and mounted the counter.

"The bathrooms are locked and I have to take a shit!" I insisted.

I awkwardly squatted over the sink.

"Don't do it in here! That's disgusting!" Virge pleaded.

"Too late!" I said. "Get out of here and give me some privacy!"

Virge and Freddy quickly left the room in revulsion, cursing under their breath.

I was wiping my ass with coarse paper towels after giving birth to a brown anaconda when two figures thrust themselves against the outside of the window, just inches from me. I yelped and launched myself off of the counter. Freddy and Virge heard the squawk and the thud and immediately reappeared in the room. I was lying on the floor with my pants around my ankles.

"What happened?!" Virge asked in alarm.

Just then, the figures were back at the window. It was a boy and girl locked in a passionate embrace.

"They're kissing!" said Virge, stating the obvious.

"Shit!" I said. "I thought it was the cops!"

Freddy and Virge chortled quietly. I didn't appreciate their boorish mirth, but I must have been a sight to see. I frantically pulled my pants back on.

Freddy had a few empty containers, including an empty cash box, and I had the art supplies. It was a meager haul. We grabbed more tempera paint on the way out. As we exited the back gate of the school onto the bike trail, Virge blurted "Look!" A squad car was pulling into the parking lot in front of the school with all of its lights off. Yes, there were motion sensors in the school, but it took the cops over thirty minutes to respond.

I wondered who would find the giant errant turd. A teacher? A student? The cop? I hoped it would be the cop. Maybe my nighttime deposits were useful after all!

ANATOMY OF A BREAK-IN

The summer of 1980 came and went. So did fall. Before we knew it, it was December. The previous month saw one of us get popped for shoplifting. It was only a matter of time, and it was me. As ugly as it was, I was still game for one more big break-in. I suppose it was my way of thumbing my nose at the cops. They recorded my fingerprints when I was taken into custody for shoplifting, but I always wore gloves during our burglaries. My attitude was basically "fuck the police."

Freddy claimed that he needed tools. Power tools. God knows for what. These kind of items were too big and bulky to hide under our clothes in a raid on a retail store. He suggested that Yorba Linda Middle School would be a cornucopia of power tools. The huge room where the shop classes were given would be full of them. This was Jake Faris' school at the time, and he had a wood shop class. Jake had been wise to our criminal activities for several months, so we didn't feel like a few questions would corrupt him more. He could tell us where all the good stuff was kept.

According to Jake, the best power tools were kept in metal cabinets on one wall of the classroom. The teacher put the keys in his desk, and if the little office inside the classroom could be breached, the keys would be easy to find. Freddy and Virge and I began to plan our most foolhardy heist to date.

Freddy had made the transition from Catholic school to public school in the seventh grade. He knew Yorba Linda Middle School well because he had attended it. Virge had been schooled there, too. They knew the shop room, and Jake could apprise us of any changes that had been made over the intervening years.

Freddy knew that there was a three-foot-square hatch on top of the classroom. It was secured with a padlock, but Freddy's bolt cutters would make short work of the lock. We could drop down on a rope and pillage the place. If we had time, we would also scale the science building, disassemble the air conditioning unit on top, and crawl through the ducts until we were inside the building. Using my Corolla for this felony was out. I didn't want to take the chance of it being identified. We'd use our bicycles.

Freddy and I rode our bikes to the junior high one afternoon to case the joint. It was already Christmas vacation for the students and no one was around. An enormous pine grew within a couple of feet of the shop's roof. Freddy figured he could climb the tree and then drop a rope to Virge and me who would tie the bag of burglary tools and empty sacks to it, which he could then hoist to the rooftop. The roof of the science building looked just as easy to access. There was a cinder block wall just under the eaves that we could climb. The top of the wall was just four feet from the roof.

As Freddy and I stood outside the shop, I pointed to a drainage ditch perhaps twenty yards to the east. "We can leave here on our bikes using the ditch!" I said. "No one will see us!" Freddy nodded politely. Getting in and out of any of the concrete drainage ditches in town was no easy task. Especially with bikes and heavy bags of loot. There was a chain-link fence on top and then a drop of ten feet. Nonetheless, it seemed like a prudent measure, at least to me. After all, we had to cover our escape somehow. Three young men riding their bikes in a line in the wee dark hours of the morning, all dressed in black and transporting multiple bulging bags would definitely get reported if we were seen. And, we wouldn't be covering a small distance. The junior high was one and a half miles away from home base. A mile and a half in. A mile and a half back. On ten-speeds.

Back at the Filipos' place, we confirmed to Virge that everything was "go." We chose 2:00 a.m. the coming Sunday night for the burglary. Sunday night was always especially dead, no matter where you were in town. Freddy collected the tools he thought we would need—a variety of screwdrivers, metal shears, a hammer, a crowbar, and the bolt cutters. We also set aside the darkest clothing we could find. Black shirts, our darkest jeans, and dark beanies. We didn't have any rope, but we did find several brand-new packages of light-duty cotton clothesline in the Filipos' garage. We secretly braided the lines together until we had a hundred feet of triply thick cordage. We were all sure that it would hold our weight, but there were no guarantees. Freddy also fitted a double-filter dust mask with a pool hose, just in case whoever crawled through the air ducts in the science building encountered massive amounts of dust or noxious substances. Safety first, right?

Sunday night, 2:00 a.m., zero hour. Freddy and I met Virge behind Freddy's garage. Freddy extracted the bag of break-in tools from under a bush and we checked that we had the necessary loot sacks and that we were all dressed in appropriately shadowy attire. Virge's jacket was a little more showy than we had hoped, but his wardrobe didn't include anything darker, and it was cold.

We pedaled down two sections of the bike trail until it began to veer too far from our target. We left the trail and went onto quiet neighborhood streets at Santa Fe Street. A short time later, we arrived at Valley View Avenue where we could see the school across the street. "Let's go!" Freddy said cheerfully.

There was not a single car to be seen on the usually busy Valley View. We hurried across and onto the school's vast unfenced ball field and cycled directly to the shop building dead ahead. After a little hushed debate about where we should hide the bikes, Freddy was adamant that if we laid them flat under the big pine there that the dark shadow of the tree would be enough— we needed our getaway vehicles to be close at hand. Without saying another word, Freddy, the most nimble of us, climbed the tree with the coil of rope around his neck and shoulder. He soon appeared on the roof's edge above us. Down came the rope, which Virge used to tie around the handles of our tool bag and the empty sacks. Freddy hoisted them to the roof.

Now came the hard parts of this endeavor. Getting up the tree, onto the roof, and into the shop down the rope. I didn't know if my upper body strength was up to the task. Virge was next up the tree. With some difficulty, he was able to shimmy up the trunk to the branches near the roof, which was a vertical climb of perhaps ten feet. I noticed that he was having trouble making the transition from the tree to the roof. He soon disappeared.

My turn. Shimmying up the rough bark was a challenge. I got up about six feet, and one of my thighs slipped on the broad trunk. I dropped to the grass below. "C'mon!" said Virge impatiently, peering at me from the roof's edge. I had better luck on my next attempt, and I was quickly in the tightly arranged branches and thick clusters of needles. The roof was two feet away from where I was in the tree. I had to jump. Luckily, I made it without getting snagged in the branches, but my landing created a loud thump as well as a noisy slide on my hands and knees in the loose gravel on the rooftop.

"Shhhh!" Freddy and Virge admonished in chorus.

Now I was covered with sticky tree sap, as were Freddy and Virge. My two accomplices were kneeling by the heavy metal hatch. It was indeed locked, but locked on the outside with a common padlock. With his first try, Freddy snipped clean through the shank with his twenty-four-inch bolt cutters. The lid of the hatch was quietly lifted to reveal a pitch-black void below. There was about two feet of metal ladder welded to the inside casement of the hatch, but none of us was eager to drop another eight feet to the floor without aid. I suggested to Freddy that we tie the rope to the metal rungs of the ladder, but this created difficulty getting safely onto the rope. Instead, Freddy walked twenty feet to the pine tree and somehow secured the braided clothesline around the trunk. The rope was dropped through the hole and landed on the concrete below with a satisfying "plop." Freddy mounted the little ladder inside the hatch, grabbed the line, and slowly disappeared into the darkness. Our bags and equipment were then lowered on the rope. Virge was next. He was even slower. Once I was on the rope and headed down, I cleared the ladder clumsily and was hanging free in space, swinging back and forth. I almost lost my grip.

All of us were in. There was enough light coming in from narrow windows at the top of the outside facing wall that our flashlights would only be needed for small spaces. Virge and Freddy were standing at the far wall examining the metal cabinets there. I began looking around the room to see what might have been left in the open that was worth grabbing. All I saw were gas cylinders for welding and some big bins of wood and metal.

"I'm not going out that way," I announced as quietly but audibly as I could. "There's no way I can do a free-hand climb up that rope!"

Freddy checked the door to the field outside.

"We can unlock this door from this side!"

I was relieved.

"Are there motion sensors?" I asked with some concern.

"I dunno," was Freddy's answer. "We need to make this quick. Ten minutes, tops."

Freddy was now trying to jimmy the door to the teacher's office, which was a tiny room within the shop enclosed by steel panels and wire-reinforced safety glass. His screwdrivers and crowbar were having no effect, and the keys to the cabinets where the good stuff was stashed were in the desk inside.

"Whoompf! Whoompf! Whoompf!"

Freddy began striking the glass on the door with the crowbar.

"Shhh!" Virge hissed in alarm.

"Stop!" I said. "That's too loud!"

Freddy didn't respond and kept whacking at the glass. He'd only created some cracks. He then grabbed his hammer from the tool bag and started beating the glass more furiously.

"Stop! Stop!" I cried with more urgency.

The hammer worked. Freddy had created a hole large enough to slide his hand through, but not with a glove on. He poked away the wire in the hole, reached in with his bare hand and unlocked the door from the inside, cutting his wrist in the process. Within just a few seconds he had found the keys in the desk (Jake had told us exactly what drawer to look in). The key ring was loaded with keys. Freddy had an idea of what a key to metal cabinets should look like, but he had to try a half dozen of them. I worried that he wouldn't find the necessary key at all.

"Hurry up!" I whispered harshly.

The key was found, and it opened all of the storage on the wall, but precious minutes had ticked by. Freddy found everything he had hoped for—a plethora of used power tools. He began stuffing them into the biggest duffel bag we brought, without regard to their condition. Virge was looking through the cabinets and continued to find things.

"Saber saw. You want it?!"

"Yes," responded Freddy.

"Reciprocating saw. Want it?!"

"Yes."

"Jigsaw?!"

"Yes."

"Impact drill?!"

"Yes."

The big duffel was quickly filled to capacity, and they were sure there was nothing else worth nicking. They joined me at the tall wood cabinets lining the inside wall, where I had just popped several of the doors open with the crowbar. I had found something unexpected and spectacular.

"A jar of money!" I murmured excitedly.

"No way!" said Virge.

There, on a shelf, was a large glass jar. It was stuffed to the brim with bills.

"Open it!" Freddy demanded.

I tried unscrewing the metal lid, but it was cinched down so tight I thought it had been glued on. The fact that I couldn't get a good grip on the glass with my slick black leather gloves wasn't helping.

"I can't get the lid off!"

"Let me try!" insisted Freddy.

He had no luck, either.

"Here!" I said in frustration, taking the jar away from Virge who was now holding it against his barrel-shaped chest and fecklessly wrenching at the lid.

I took both of my gloves off (big mistake!), grasped the glass as firmly as I could and twisted the lid with all of my strength. It came free and I looked inside.

"There must be hundreds of dollars in here!" I said in astonishment.

"Whoa!" responded Virge. "Take all of it!"

The money was dumped into one of our smaller bags, and we grabbed our other sacks of spoils. Freddy was right about the door to the outside. He easily unlocked it and ventured out of the classroom. He looked around for a few seconds, even going to the end of the building to scan the front parking lot, but didn't see anything alarming. Despite his earlier admonition that we should only be inside the school for ten minutes, we had actually been inside for twenty. Still no cops. Either there were no alarm sensors, or the police were slow to respond. The night was still young, and there was one more thing we wanted to do.

We gathered our bikes and walked to the science classrooms two buildings deeper into the interior of the campus. The cafeteria was just beyond the science building. A dozen of the usual thermoplastic-coated fiberglass picnic tables were outside. There was a breezeway between the buildings that gave us a good view of the front drive to the school, so we lingered at one of the tables for fifteen more minutes to see if the authorities would arrive. Nothing. On to our next task.

Freddy and I showed Virge the wall we had found that would allow us to get onto the roof of the science building. Virge briefly looked at the wall, which formed an empty cubby at the back of the structure. "Let's do it!" he said.

We brought the bikes and the loot into the cubbyhole. Freddy was the first to climb onto the roof, and did so with ease. Virge scrambled up the wall and stood on top. I handed him the bag of break-in tools and a few empty bags. He then passed them to Freddy and hoisted himself onto the roof. I followed and found it a much easier matter than clambering up a tree, but lifting myself the additional four feet onto the roof was a little bit tricky. I almost fell.

The air conditioning unit wasn't hard to find. It was a massive cluster of square edifices in the middle of the roof. We did a walk around it, giving it a good looking over, and decided that the biggest grille had to be the main air intake. Freddy and Virge began taking out all of the screws on this grate, and it was off in a couple of minutes. Freddy peered inside using his square plastic flashlight.

"It goes down about ten feet and stops," he told us.

"It can't just stop!" I countered. "The air has to go somewhere! Maybe it's a tee."

"We won't know unless someone goes down there," Virge added.

The duct opening showed us that Virge and I were just too large to navigate the sheet-metal tunnel. Freddy would have to go in. He was considerably smaller.

"Looks like it could get pretty dusty," he said.

We didn't want to put Freddy at respiratory risk, so we hauled out the dust mask and pool hose contraption he had constructed. Freddy pulled the mask over his face and proceeded to squeeze into the duct. Virge and I fed the air hose in behind him. With considerable effort, he crawled to where he thought the tunnel ended.

"It's a tee!" he called back to us, muffled by the mask. "It goes left and right, but it gets narrower!"

"Can you go further?" Virge inquired.

"I think so."

The pool hose was only ten feet long, so Freddy would have to continue without it.

"No more hose!" I informed him.

Freddy took off the respirator and dropped it with a soft "clunk" on the metal crawlway. He looked down the duct to his right and saw nothing but blackness. When he looked to the left, he saw pale light shining through a register to a classroom.

"I can see light!" he called.

"Great!" I said. "Can you get down there?!"

"I dunno. I'll try."

In the beam of our flashlight, we could see Freddy curl up and begin wiggling and twisting, trying to get his feet into the left duct. It took a few minutes, but he soon got himself onto his back and aligned in the new direction. He slowly inched away until he disappeared.

"I'm going to kick out this grate!" we heard him say, his voice now barely audible. "Go to the door on the other side of the building. I'll meet you there."

We could hear the faint sounds of his feet bashing at the metal air conditioning register.

It looked like we were in! When Virge and I arrived at the prescribed door, we tapped on a window there. Freddy was already out of the ducting and let us into the building. The combination of soft moonlight and artificial campus lighting shining through the big windows allowed us to move around without flashlights.

Hmmm... What could we use from a science lab? There were two rooms, one a standard classroom with desks and chairs, the other was divided up with long free-standing counters with sinks. There were also many cabinets along the walls. It was the lab portion. Between the two rooms was an open storage area. It was here that Freddy had kicked out the register and dropped into the building.

"Whoooaaa! Look at that!" I said on seeing the vent. "Did you get hurt?"

"Not really," Freddy responded matter-of-factly. "I cut my legs a little."

The air conditioning vent never came away from the wall and what remained was splayed out in every direction. The hole in it was so small, I was amazed Freddy was able to squeeze through it.

We fanned out. Virge went into the classroom area to look around. I went into the lab and started going through cabinets. Freddy rifled through the chemicals and equipment in the storage area.

We found some beakers and test tubes that looked useful and stuffed them into our bags. Freddy grabbed a few containers of chemicals that he recognized. There were brand-new microscopes in the storeroom, too. I stepped out of the storage area into the classroom where Virge was milling about.

"Do you want a microscope?" I asked.

"Nah," Virge replied.

Just then, a figure passed by the classroom windows. I clearly saw a tan Brea Police uniform.

"A cop!" I whispered frantically. "The cops are here!"

We turned our heads to regard the sound of a hand testing the door to the classroom. We had been careful to close it and lock it behind us. The officer continued on.

I immediately went to Freddy who was now in the lab section of the classrooms going through the cabinets.

"Cops! " I told him, freaking out.

Freddy's big blue eyes opened wide and he looked genuinely concerned for once.

"Really?" he answered. "Where?"

"One just walked up to the door and tested it to see if it was open! He walked right past the windows in here! Didn't you see him?!"

"No!"

"We need to stay completely quiet and not move around."

We waited, breathlessly watching the windows. Fifteen minutes passed and nothing more was seen or heard.

"We need to make a run for it," Freddy finally declared.

"Shit!" I said. "How do we know that cop isn't still out there?"

"He was checking to see if anything was open," Freddy told us. "They do that when the sensors go off. If nothing's open and nothing looks suspicious they leave."

"What about the bikes?" Virge interjected. "And all the bags? Do you think the cop found them?"

"We'll find out," Freddy said.

Still clutching our sacks of meager but hard-won goods, we quickly and quietly exited the classrooms and ran for the niche where our bikes and shop loot were hidden. Everything was still there—why hadn't the cop found them?! We took a moment to sling the bags over our bikes and bodies. Freddy took the enormous duffel of stolen tools and slipped the single strap around his neck and shoulders. I put a bag on the top tube of my bike and held another slung over one shoulder. Virge did the same. It was going to be an awkward and cumbersome ride home.

As we took off across the ball field, I called to my wobbling comrades.

"The ditch! Let's use the ditch!"

I still thought it was worth the hassle to get into the drainage ditch, even with bikes and unwieldy cargo. At least we couldn't be seen. I didn't remember that we no longer had any rope to lower everything down. Virge and Freddy ignored me. They were getting an uncomfortable lead on me, too.

We retraced the route we had taken to get to the school. Virge and I stopped frequently to readjust our loads. Freddy was so far ahead of us that he could no longer be seen. We reached the bottom of Freddy's driveway after twenty minutes of pumping the pedals. I took one of the bags Virge carried so that it could be hidden in the grove for a while, and he took off for home.

I found Freddy on the driveway at the top of the hill. I also noticed that the garage door, which was usually closed at night, was standing wide open. This didn't look good.

"Was the garage open when we left?" I asked him.

"I don't think so," Freddy responded with a hint of nervousness in his hushed voice. "I'm going to stash the power tools in the grove so we can get them later."

Freddy disappeared into the orange grove with the bulging duffel bag of spoils. I walked my bike to the back of the garage where the bikes typically stood. A few minutes later, Freddy was back from the grove and putting his ten-speed away. I waited for him on the driveway catercorner to the front of the open garage.

Without warning, the door to the house inside of the garage flew open and Arnie came storming out! Straight for me! *Ho-leee SHIT!*

"What are you boys doing out here?!" he demanded.

"Nothing!" I said sheepishly, trying to stay calm.

"Where's Fredrick?!"

"Here I am," Freddy called as he appeared from the back of the garage.

"What are you doing?!" his father repeated sternly.

"Riding bikes," Freddy answered soberly.

"Riding bikes?! At this time of night?! Why are you boys both dressed in black?"

"No reason."

"Get in the house! Both of you! We're going to talk about this in the morning! Go to bed!"

Now what?! How were we going to get out of this one?! Freddy and I made a bee-line for the bedroom. As we bedded down, I asked my comrade what he thought had tipped off his dad. Freddy could only shrug. We both agreed on a common "bike riding" story in case we were separated when we were questioned in the morning. I soon fell into an uneasy sleep, exhausted. Sunrise would bring hell, and in more ways than I could have imagined.

CONSEQUENCES

Freddy and I were rudely raised from our catatonic slumbers by Arnie early the next morning. Arnie should have been on his way to work that Monday, but he wanted to interrogate us at the earliest possible opportunity.

We met Arnie and Midge at the dining room table where we were given the third degree. Thankfully, we weren't grilled separately. Freddy and I repeated what we had agreed upon as our story: we couldn't sleep, and we went outside to do some nocturnal bike riding. We had never done this before and thought it would be fun. Where did we go? Just up and down Rose Drive, Loie Street, Prentiss Drive. Not far. Why were we both wearing black? It was just a coincidence. We hadn't intended to wear nothing but black.

Freddy's mother and father were incredulous. "Are you sure there's not something you should be telling us?" Arnie finally inquired. Nope. That was it, and we were sticking to our story. When all was said and done, we were put on notice. Arnie and Midge would be watching.

The next day, fourteen-year-old Jake Faris came by. We talked privately in the bedroom Freddy and I shared. Jake could get nothing out of his brother about the junior high heist, and he had some important information to share. As fate would have it, Jake had a first-period wood shop class the day after the burglary. "The police were there," he informed me. "And my shop teacher was crying."

I wasn't buying the bit about the teacher crying. Jake was just adding this for effect. The police being there was not a big surprise. But, there was one really bad part to Jake's report. The police showed a list to the first-period shop students.

"Do you know anybody on this list?" an officer asked Jake.

Jake scanned the twenty or so names on the paper and clearly saw mine among them.

"No," Jake responded to the cop flatly.

(Good boy, Jake!)

Of course, none of the other students had a clue who I was, so the police came up short with this little tactic.

"Did you guys take the money in the jar?" Jake asked me.

"The jar in the wooden cabinets? Yeah, yeah. We did," I admitted.

"Did you touch the jar with your bare hands?"

"Yeah! I did!"

"They took fingerprints off of that jar!"

"Shit! You're kidding me!"

"No! They took fingerprints!"

This was a huge, hairy problem. The police recorded my fingerprints after taking me into custody for shoplifting just a month earlier. How could I have been so stupid?! Stupid! Stupid! Stupid!

"The money in that jar was for a class project," Jake continued.

I felt bad now, in addition to being badly scared.

"I'm sorry, Jake. We didn't know."

Freddy had hidden our two-thirds of the cash from the jar in a fanny pack there in our bedroom. I retrieved it and gave Jake the seven dollars he had contributed to the shop project. The total cash take had been just over a hundred dollars. Pathetic.

"Here's your money back, Jake."

"It doesn't matter. We can't do the project now."

"I'm sorry. There's nothing we can do now. We didn't know."

Next to visit was Virge. We talked about who left fingerprints at the school. I reminded him that I had handled the money jar with my bare hands, and that Freddy had used his bare hand to reach through the broken safety glass to unlock the door to the teacher's office. "I saw Freddy wipe off the knob with his shirttail!" Virge insisted. I hadn't seen this. If it was true, it meant I was the only one who left clear evidence. I could only hope that many other people had handled that jar and that there were innumerable fingerprints all over the glass.

I also told Virge that his brother had come by to tell me that he had seen the police taking fingerprints off of the jar, and that he was shown a list of known offenders with my name on it. I was sure I was doomed. It was just a matter of time before I was arrested. Virge and Freddy would be implicated too, but I was going to do some time behind bars. I had recently turned eighteen. I was an adult and I would be prosecuted as an adult.

For the next couple of weeks I was in a constant state of fear and apprehension. I wasn't good company. What was taking the cops so long? Why hadn't a squad car or two appeared at the Filipos' house to take me away? How would my arrest effect everyone? How was I going to explain my arrest to my parents? During this waiting game, I was desperate to throw the authorities off in some way. If I were to just move to another place, that might make it a little harder for them to pin me down. I took some time off from work to visit with my parents in Central California. This would allow me to hide out for a while and mull over my prospects. I received a letter from Virge while I was away. According to him, "A squad car appeared at the top of the Filipos' driveway with all of its lights flashing. Everyone was in a panic!" This may have been my ride. Then again, it might just be some bullshit Virge had thought up as psychological torture—penance for the trouble I had brought down on the three of us. Everyone was in a panic? That means someone saw the police car. If Arnie and Midge had been home, the police would have knocked on the door and talked to them. How could the Farises have seen the squad car? Even pressed against the back fence that divided the Faris and Filipino properties, the Farises would be hard pressed to see anything with orange trees and a garage between them and the driveway. The more I thought about it, the more it seemed like Virge was just being a prick.

I returned to Yorba Linda a week later. The nauseating specter of arrest still hung over me. My relationships with Virge and Freddy had also soured so much that I approached a friend at work who was having roommate problems and wanted to find a new apartment. All he needed was a new roommate to share the cost.

Within a couple of weeks, I left the Filipos' and was in an apartment in Anaheim with my coworker. But this wasn't enough. I was still sure that it was only a matter of time before I heard that particular knock on the front door. After two months in the apartment, I found a new roommate for my work friend and moved half way up California to the town where my sister and her family lived.

I never did get arrested for the Yorba Linda Middle School heist. A whole new chapter in my life began. I lived for a year in the San Joaquin Valley and then went back to Orange County to go to college. I got my life straightened out and became a model citizen. Leaving Yorba Linda was one of the best decisions I ever made! ▪

· CHAPTER 10 ·

HALLOWEENERS

 Pumpkin snatching. I must admit that it sounds somewhat off-beat, but this prank's history is well rooted in my protracted childhood. In October of 1978, I was able to visit with Virge at his home in Yorba Linda just over a year after I had moved out of Southern California. I had weaseled my parents into allowing me to visit Virge to help with his semi-annual Halloween party. The visit and party were great, but getting out of three days of school in the hick haven where my parents had moved us—in addition to the weekend—now, that was sheer bliss.

Virge's party, like his last in '76, was quite an undertaking. We went all out to supply a spectacular atmosphere. We constructed a large crawl-through maze of cardboard boxes, employed a strobe light and a blood spitting grim reaper marionette, and decorated with leafy tree limbs, sheets, corn stalks, and jack-o-lanterns. We transformed Virge's garage into a colorful, old-fashioned embodiment of the holiday. I can still smell the linen, leaves, and carved pumpkins. It was too bad that most of the guests were squirrelly, obnoxious, and unappreciative assholes. Something told me that Virge was scraping the bottom of the barrel when it came to coming up with enough "friends" to invite to a party.

The party had been on Sunday night, October 28, and on Monday I cleaned up most of the mess. I was the only person at the Faris residence not at work or school that day. I was still in a cleaning mood on Tuesday, so I attacked Virge's room. What a dump! Despite its challenge, I eventually conquered it with the help of a vacuum and Lady Madonna by the Beatles on K-EARTH 101*. Virge was surprised but extremely grateful on return from school that day.

By Wednesday, I had become bored with my stay but was hopeful of more exciting events now that it was Halloween day. Virge sympathized with my boredom and the incredible cleaning display that sprang from it.

He was game for more than just a final crack at trick-or-treating, too. We were old for that kind of thing, really. I was sixteen and Virge was fifteen, shortly to be sixteen. We discussed pranks: soaping windows, lighting off firecrackers on someone's doorstep, popping confetti balloons right outside someone's lit window and running (as we had done the Halloween two years earlier), but nothing seemed novel or even slightly exciting.

I gave the situation some thought and mentioned that we might steal pumpkins from a stand.

"Too dangerous," Virge mumbled.

"How about taking jack-o-lanterns off of people's front porches?" I offered.

Virge's eyes began to glow.

"Yeah… Yeah!" he yawped.

Mean? Perhaps. The basic urge was to vandalize. At least we would spare children seeing their creations rot. I know my jack-o-lanterns persisted well into November after their initial Halloween glory, decomposing in full view on the compost heap. It was depressing. We'd spare Yorba Linda children this sight. We would descend upon their homes and whisk the pumpkins away, semi-ceremoniously scattering their fruits upon the night.

I guess this was just another instance where I turned to dumb nighttime activities for kicks, not unlike the hood ornament collection that Virge and I started just before I moved out of the area. I didn't recognize that I was just an angry kid acting out through vandalism and thievery.

Nighttime descended on the Halloween of 1978 quickly, and Virge and I were soon escorting his brother, Jake (then eleven), to the hoots and haunts of residential Yorba Linda with costumes donned. Virge wore the Star Wars Tusken Raider mask I had made for him for the party. The only additional costuming Virge had was a burlap serape he had thrown together at the last minute. (I can also attest that he worked himself into a snit because he had to go to more than one nursery in search of the appropriate material.) I wore my hot, homemade Darth Vader costume, complete with elevator shoes, armor, cape, and dorky Don Post Studios mask.

We had no problem scaring smaller kids on the street. Jake, like his brother, also wore a "last moment" costume that consisted of one of his father's shirts (or was it an overcoat?) and the rubber "old-man" mask Virge had used for his party in '76, and that I had used for my own party in '75.

A section of the bike trail a half block from the Filipo property off of Rose Drive (1979 photo)

With a good haul of candy and some very uplifting comments on our costumes, we went back to Virge's to rest. It was my last night before leaving for home.

When Virge's mother and father bedded down around ten that night, it was only a matter of minutes before we were out on the street. During junior high, we'd drop a bunk bed ladder out of Virge's window to exit the house. This process was so tedious and noisy—not to mention stupid—that by high school we were leaving via the side door near the garage. Judging from the enormous stock of condoms in Mr. Faris' nightstand drawer, which Virge and I once used for giant amorphous water balloons, I believe Mr. Faris was a real horn-dog for his age. Going past the parents' bedroom door to get to our exit was never a problem. It was almost always closed. However, we were still extremely quiet, and for years of sneaking out, Virge and I were never caught leaving his house. Not once.

Out on Virge's street, the cold air was tremendously invigorating. We entered the bike trail.

"Remember that place?" I asked Virge, pointing to a rift of thick green foliage behind some enormous oil tanks.

"That's the wild berry trench that we fell into while trying to escape that man… you threw the light bulb from his front porch light against his door, and he came out! Remember?"

Virge smiled.

"Yeah… I remember."

In one of our earliest stunts, probably in the fall of 1975, we had noisily jumped from Virge's window and beat a path to the field of dirt-clod-covered ground we now faced. Virge disengaged a light bulb from someone's entryway socket on Laro Lane, while I waited in the dark of some avocado trees in the field below. "Pop!" the bulb shattered against the casement of the people's front door after a well-aimed heave by Virge, who was standing on their front lawn. I began approaching him thinking nothing would happen. Virge was now crouched behind some shrubs on the edge of the lawn. Suddenly, the door of the house flew open, and a man hopped onto the landing! There was some cursing I couldn't quite make out. Perhaps I couldn't hear it because of the wind whistling in my ears as I ran. The last

The trench full of berry vines was just off the bike trail
and behind the oil tanks shown here (1980 photo).

thing I saw before turning to run was Virge leaping out from behind those bushes in full view of his angry victim. And Virge was *running*! He caught up with me in no time, and we tripped and stumbled through the big clods of the field in a flagrant retreat to what we hoped was the safety of darkness. I came to a screeching halt.

"What the hell is this?" I asked somewhat rhetorically under my breath.

"Raspberry vines!" Virge informed me, panting. "It's not a very wide ditch! Let's jump it! Over here! It's narrow!"

"Well, go! Hurry!" I cried.

I expected Virge's victim was working his way down through the field to our eventual capture. Almost simultaneously, we strained huge broad jumps. I knew I was doomed to agony while still in midair. It was a just punishment. Both Virge and I landed in the middle of what turned out to be a veritable tiger trap of thorny berry canes. The vines that appeared to spread out across a narrow ditch and then solid ground actually hovered over a wide, deep trench. I fell through, up to my waist in sharp stickers. Virge just fell, sprawled on top of the netting of needles face down.

Slowly, tenaciously, we crawled out of the mess. The man didn't follow us as we had suspected he might, and on the other side of the berry patch we cursed, pulling at the thorns in our clothing. The black sweater I wore would forever contain painful reminders of that night. We went home in awe of our stupidity, laughing about our "sticky situation."

Virge chuckled as I reminded him of that episode.

"It seems like a long time ago already," he said.

The area through which we now walked was dark enough for an easy pumpkin snatch, but houses were not easily accessible near the big eucalyptus trees that cast their hiding shadows. We went up to the first intersecting street, Prospect Avenue, and turned right, off the bike trail. We were now on Hillcrest Circle. In the cul-de-sac there, we soon found the object of our search. Although most of the houses we had passed were surprisingly devoid of jack-o-lanterns, one residence had two big darkened ones perched on cornices near the front door.

In turn, we approached our prize, snatched it up, and ran gleefully to the corner a block away. On Prospect, we congratulated one another on a snag well done and made haste for the bike trail with the weighty, deeply ridged squashes. With a little debating, we finally decided that Santa Fe Street, further up the trail, would be a more "fruitful" area. We left the pumpkins on the path side.

Going east from Santa Fe down Orange Drive, we came upon a house on the corner of Tucana Street with its porch light still on. Below the light, in the entry, was a bundle of corn stalks and two pumpkins, which we quickly and carefully snatched. I got a measly elongated specimen, and Virge got a large, round squat one. Both were uncarved. Tsk! Tsk! Lazy people! We went back to Santa Fe.

On Santa Fe, we were out in the open, and when a car passed through a nearby intersection, we nervously ditched our purloined pumpkins in a small plot with orange trees. With a little more half-hearted searching to the east, we found a disappointing lack of jack-o-lanterns, so we went back to the little plot. As we approached our stash there, we could see another car coming, so we hid behind the low wall and trees there. Luckily, the driver didn't see us, and even more luckily, it wasn't a patrol car. We were always wary of patrol cars. Technically, we were breaking a city curfew law as well as engaging in mischievous mischief.

Virge and I packed up our loot and walked back down the bike trail to our two carved prizes.

"Let's smash 'em!" Virge grunted barbarically.

I didn't expect we'd keep the carved ones.

"Okay!" I said.

Rather like Neanderthals lifting huge stones over our heads to mash an unsuspecting groundhog, we hurled the grinning pumpkins against the bike path's asphalt.

"Plomp! Clop!"

We stomped the larger pieces, giggling with glee.

"So much for those jack-o-lanterns!" I smiled. "Want these candles?!"

"Nah!" Virge said. "Let's go."

Next, we went to Prentiss, the small street that was a spur off of Virge's street. Everything was dead quiet. We found little in the way of front-porch booty on Prentiss, but stumbled upon a trash can with brightly-colored refuse beneath its lid… something orange. Pumpkins! We decided to smash what we found in the can on the bike trail nearby. Another section of the path was only a half block away. We each took one pumpkin and scurried off.

At the bike trail, we again ecstatically dashed, tromped, and kicked the fruits. And, on the next trip back to the garbage can, there were more pumpkins still! Now we took two each, though there were more yet!

"Clop! Whunk! Plop! Whack!"

The pumpkins were smashed.

We made another trip for ammo. Nestled in the oily paper and rubbish were three more pumpkins. Back to the trail. Virge smashed one, and I smashed one.

"This is the last one!" Virge announced.

"We each get to stomp it!" I hooted mercilessly.

"Whomp!"

The pumpkin broke in two, and each of us jumped on a slippery half.

The wake of our savage fun was incredible. Pumpkin shards everywhere! Seeds and slimy, stringy innards stretched for yards. What a mess! I don't know when I had more fun destroying something. Nine pumpkins, some small, most medium size, were scattered in every direction. I know we both felt a certain amount of satisfaction. We snuck back into bed feeling rather accomplished. What a night!

The next month, after I had returned home, I received a letter from Virge in which he mentioned the pumpkin thievery and vandalism.

"Yes, it was fun for some reason—really fun," he wrote.

I revisited Virge at Christmas time, and I found he still had the uncarved pumpkins from the Tucana Street house on his back porch.

"What are you going to do with these?" I asked him. "Are you going to make a pie or something?"

"Can't let them go to waste after all that work!" he said.

I lifted the tall skinny one I had snatched. It had "69¢" written on top in black felt-tip pen. I pointed at the price for Virge.

"And after you paid so much for them, too!"

MORE PUMPKIN LUST

Two Halloweens later, '79's being spent sick in bed, I was ready for pumpkin snatching again—for old time's sake. October 1980 found me at the Filipos', and some of the thievery that took place just the previous summer paled in comparison to the ordinary "snatch." Although Freddy and Virge had both shown interest in a large-scale snatch or full-blown pumpkin raid at the beginning of the month, they later found the idea silly, and neither came through in the end.

One afternoon, I went to a house in Placentia to retrieve a huge, home-grown pumpkin that my father had sent down from Central California with a former neighbor for my Halloween. I was reminded of a dark summer's eve just a couple months earlier when Jake Faris and I got stoned in Freddy's orange grove. We went down several sections of the bike trail to a place where I had previously seen pumpkins on the vine. I noisily and conspicuously climbed over a chain-link and rail fence there to get to the vegetables in question.

"Awww Maaan! These got rotten!" I said, picking up one of the musty concave shells.

"Leave 'em!" Jake whispered, concerned we would be discovered, "Hurry."

I grinned foolishly.

"Let's smash 'em!" I said.

"Okay," Jake responded. "But let's go!"

Down the bike trail, we joyously ran across Prospect, hurling our pumpkins in the air as we crossed. Their burst on the pavement ignited a laughing jag in both of us, and in our stupor, it lasted all the way home.

Ah, this story does repeat itself—again and again. Yeah! Why not again?! Steal some excellent pumpkins this time, but not destroy them—make them into great jack-o-lanterns!

The "Pumpkin Patch" was a large open marketplace near the corner of Palm Drive and Yorba Linda Boulevard in Placentia. When I saw the sea of pumpkins there and that the lot had a field and an orange grove bordering its far side, I immediately knew it would be possible, if risky, to steal pumpkins. I was basically interested in the challenge it posed, but also would have liked to take the biggest, roundest pumpkin on the lot.

Earlier in October, Virge and Freddy went with Jake and I to the Pumpkin Patch to check it out. Stealing pumpkins for its challenge was good enough for them at the time, but on casing the place that afternoon, we discovered that there was a multitudinous string of elevated lights that were left on over the pumpkins at night. And, on closer scrutiny, we found what appeared to be a bean-bag chair for a nighttime watchman on the back of the lot. Freddy and I had planned to park on Palm Drive with the orange grove between my car and the lot. We'd then go through the grove,

The "Pumpkin Patch" on Yorba Linda Boulevard in the city of Placentia (mid 1980s photo)

wait for a break in Yorba Linda Boulevard traffic, hop a small chain-link fence, and get a pumpkin or two. Now our plans were canceled.

By the middle of the month, any remarks I made to Freddy or Virge about snagging pumpkins from "this lot on Imperial Highway" or from "that other lot on Yorba Linda Boulevard" were met with bewildered looks at best. It was apparent that I could only rely on Jake to give me a hand. Jake had already expressed his desire to snatch pumpkins, whether off a lot or porch, it made no difference to him. He just got a charge from sneaking out at night and running around. Jake hadn't smoked out with Freddy or me in months it seemed, and this had been the only excuse he had to know liberation out on the streets late at night. When I suggested to Jake that we forget Freddy and Virge and celebrate Halloween in our own way, he was all ears. I was disappointed that Virge wouldn't be involved as he was two years earlier, but Jake's palpable excitement over a sneak-out distracted me from such thoughts. We began to bake our plot.

"In celebration of a new Halloween, we'll attempt to snatch the best pumpkins off a lot or two on Thursday night, the 30th," I told him. "We'll be out romping around that night until well after midnight when it will officially be the 31st—Halloween! The next day, you can call your school early in the morning and imitate your mother. Tell them you're sick—that you've got a sore throat. Then I can work on these special costumes for Virge and me in your room—after we meet and Virge leaves the house for school. No one will ever know that I didn't go to work and that you didn't go to school."

As crazy as it sounds, Jake had called the school as his mother on earlier occasions, and somehow the school secretary was dim-witted enough to fall for his impression every time. The plans seemed reasonable enough. However, Jake complained that he could never imitate his mother again now that his voice was changing. So, I suggested that he imitate his father. Both parents would be at work. Jake could easily make the call after his parents were gone and while Virge was taking his routine morning shower.

Jake was still apprehensive about making the call, although he agreed that he'd like the day off. I offered to make the call for him as his father, but he thought it would be best if he did it. After all, I didn't have his successful technique down. He'd pretend to go to school around 8:00 in the morning.

Virge was still as steadfast in ensuring Jake's wholesome activities as their parents, and after meeting me in a secret spot in "The Field," we would wait for Virge to depart for his classes at Fullerton Junior College and then return to Jake's house (Virge was on a program that allowed high school juniors and seniors to enroll in college courses). I'd finish the unique costumes I was making for Virge and me that we were going to spring on everyone, and Jake and I would both have a relaxing day off before a rollicking Halloween weekend. Easy peasy pumpkin squeezy.

The previous May, during Memorial Day weekend, Virge and Freddy and I became what you could call "Johnny Pumpkinseeds." We went around all the neighboring fields planting gourd, Big Max pumpkin, and Connecticut Field pumpkin seeds in hopes that plants would grow during the summer and produce fruit the next fall. One of the plantings did mature, but this amounted to only two vines from the many seeds we had planted.

During the time that Jake and I were formulating our Halloween-eve plans, Freddy and I were lucky enough to remember that we had pumpkin plants with pumpkins on them in an open part of the "raspberry ditch" field off the bike trail. We had seen small green pumpkins on the vines

The circle marks the spot of the wild-grown pumpkins in a small field near the bike trail.

earlier, and we were sure they had produced ripe fruit. So, we investigated one afternoon.

I spotted the broad pumpkin leaves interwoven with the tall, dry grass. "There it is!" I exclaimed.

We found a small, ripe warty specimen that Freddy and I had seated on a piece of discarded plywood while it was still a "greenie" a month earlier. Something strange had happened, though. Someone had propped a board against the side of our pumpkin—the side that faced a wall horseback riders would sometimes look over as they went by on a path in the field next door. It seemed obvious that someone was trying to hide what they thought was a "volunteer" plant. I suspected it was the same folks who had built a tree house nearby.

We traced a main vine that we had previously overlooked starting at its base in the damp floor of the trench to a hollow of leaves in a low avocado tree.

"Wow!" I screeched. "Look at that pumpkin!"

Under the tree, we found a well-hidden, perfectly round Big Max pumpkin. Someone had concealed it with boards. What a pleasant surprise!

Freddy and I brought Virge back later to look at it. He was as pleased as we were, and we made a pact to return the week before Halloween to retrieve it and some other less impressive fruit from the vines we had planted. We hoped no one plucked them before then.

We decided on a weeknight for our secret harvest, and I made a note for the people who tried so hard to hide our pumpkins. Using a black felt tip, on plain paper I wrote:

"Thank you for hiding our pumpkins so well! We hoped that they would mature after we worked so hard to plant them last spring. Did you think they had sprouted by chance? No! Alas, now it is time to harvest our crop. Better luck next year! Ha! Ha! Ha! And remember to watch your children carefully this All Hallows Eve or we might just eat them! Signed, The Ghosts of Halloween."

Jake, Freddy, Virge, and I all had healthy "hee-hees" over the note before encasing it in cellophane and tape. We then trudged out to the nearby field. No one was around, and the pumpkins were still there. Freddy, wearing his ever-present camouflage baseball cap, sliced their bonds with a deft stroke of his knife. We pinned the note to the vine where the biggest pumpkin had been, and all merrily loped off.

"Let me carry it!" Virge insisted.

I handed him the larger of the two pumpkins.

"Whoa! This thing is heavy!" he squawked.

"No shit!" I said, laughing.

Before we knew it, the night of the 30th fell upon Jake and me. It was time to become a stealthy spirit once again. Jake was to meet me at 11:00 p.m. at the back of the Filipos' garage to begin our pumpkin-snatching adventure. And, as that hour arose, my blood pumped fast with the anticipation of running uninhibited through the fresh night air. Freddy knew of my plans, but I'm unsure whether he knew of Jake's involvement. If he did, it was safe to assume that Freddy wouldn't tell Virge about such a trivial thing. Freddy was indifferent to my leaving but offered a pleasant, "have fun!" before getting back to the more critical matter of falling asleep.

From our darkened bedroom window, I could see Jake—or "Lizard Man," as Freddy and I had taken to calling him—milling about near the Filipos' utility sheds. Freddy and I once joked that the band *Lynyrd Skynyrd* was actually *Lizard Skinner*, as in "someone who skins their lizard" (masturbates). Jake got slapped with *Lizard Skinner* for a while, too, and later *Lizard Man* for use in mixed company. Poor Jake.

It was only 10:30 and he wasn't at the designated meeting place! I had to quell my anger at Jake's early appearance as I had done so many times the previous summer. I understood Jake's excitement, enthusiasm, and early arrivals more than Freddy did, but I still held to my roommate's belief that, "An early Lizard Man is a conspicuous Lizard Man." If Arnie or Midge were still up, which they very well could have been, Jake would be taking all the more chance of being discovered. I also felt like Jake expected me to dash from the house, even if just to end his pitiful shuffling. It was irritating, to be sure.

In any case, I successfully exited the house that night and met Jake. I informed him that we would first investigate a small, dark, out-of-the-way pumpkin stand on Yorba Linda Boulevard near an Alpha Beta. He agreed.

Using the bike trail again, we followed several sections from Rose Drive to Santa Fe and then to Orange Drive—a distance of about a mile and a half on foot. This area vividly reminded me of the snatching two years earlier.

We came to a line of enormous eucalyptus trees, and before passing them we cut through to a field with oil pumps. "Freet! Kfreeet!" the slowly bobbing lever of one pump droned quietly in the distance.

"No cars yet. We're making good time," I thought to myself. I was feeling confident, but best of all charged up and completely free. At the edge of the oil field, Jake and I quietly navigated down a steep bank and entered a dark parking lot surrounded by pines off of Liverpool Street. Soon, we were in a churchyard, and we cautiously avoided its lights by going around the buildings past a high fence. A dog barked loudly behind the fence and Jake jumped.

"Don't be so nervous!" I whispered to him. "We're right near Yorba Linda Boulevard now. There's the lot with pumpkins. You can see it from here. Let's go!"

Jake stood in the shadows of small building, not following my advance. "C'mon!" I said.

"You go… I… I'm going to wait here," came his voice with a hard swallow. I went back to his rigid silhouette and urged him more strenuously.

"Don't chicken out now! Let's go!"

"No. I can't."

"Waddayamean, 'I can't'?"

"I don't want to… You go. I'll stay here."

"Oh, man!" I said in disgust. "What a time to be a sketch-prone skiod*! I'm going. Wait here!"

I crossed a darkened lawn to Yorba Linda Boulevard. I could see the lot on the other side—and one small trailer. A dim light over its door illuminated the pumpkins. It was a local Boy Scout stand. I remembered now.

I could hear a car coming. I dropped back behind a wall and out of the light of a nearby street lamp. I was squatting like a giant toad, ready to spring out and race across the road when it was clear. I looked back at the anxious Jake—his bespectacled eyes were locked on my every move, being careful not to lose me.

"Ha! He just wanted to sneak out for the sake of sneaking out!" I concluded.

Gad! My feet were soaking wet from the grass where I crouched. The car never came—time to go. I hustled across the street to the patch of pumpkin-covered dirt. Now what? I sat on a large broken block of concrete, hidden in a fence's shadow right on the corner of the lot. Then, I heard another car coming. Before I could crane my neck to look down the road, a squad car whooshed up... then passed. He didn't see me. Whew! That was close! I surely looked suspicious! What's my next move? Get up!

I stood up and ventured onto the sidewalk. Shit! Another car! This one had already caught me in its headlights after topping a hill, so I thrust my hands into my pockets and began walking up the street, trying hard to look like someone with no particular intentions. By the time I turned onto another nearby street, the car was upon me! It turned where I had turned! I tried to look casual, unconcerned. It too passed.

"Damn it!" I thought. "I'm getting some pumpkins!" I had had enough. With renewed determination, I walked back into the lot. A few glances at the dimly lit trailer proved nothing new.

Good Lord! The pumpkins were pathetic. All of them were small—most were rotten or lopsided. I walked along the lines of orange spheres and ovals, nudging one, tapping another with the toe of my shoe.

"Hmmm," I mused, "this one looks decent." I turned the pumpkin over to find the bottom soft and dented. "Damn!"

I must have been on that lot in full view for at least five minutes, just pushing at pumpkins. Finally, I decided on two agreeably hard, round ones. I picked them up and ran across the street to Jake.

"Look at these," I told him. "These are the best ones I could find. I can get more easily, though... want more?!"

Jake didn't look too thrilled.

"Okay, we'll go," I said. "This one's yours, here."

When I handed Jake a pumpkin, I was rewarded with a definite twinkle in his eye. I wasn't sure if the twinkle was for our departure or the gift of the pumpkin.

"That was a piece of cake!" I said.

I then examined the pumpkin in my possession.

"This one looks decent."

I turned the pumpkin over to find the bottom soft and dented.

"Damn. Damn! Damn!"

The drainage ditch (1979 photo)

How any organization could sell such a god-awful product was amazing to me—this seemed like the kiss of death for the Scouts' little pumpkin stand business.

12:30 a.m. found us back at the Filipos' grove.

"It's Halloween, Jake!" I announced.

"Yeah," he said with a smile. "What do you want to do now?"

I was still full of energy.

"You know that pumpkin stand on the corner of Rose Drive and Imperial Highway that I wanted to get into so badly?" I asked.

"Yeah," Jake said, slightly amused.

"Let's go up there. I want to see if I can get some massive pumpkins."

We were off again, down through "The Field," across Bastanchury Road, and onto a dirt strip bordering the big drainage ditch that marked the border between Placentia and Yorba Linda. We were in an area we rarely traveled, but one I had frequented for lizard hunting when I was in elementary school. This place was spooky. It was well below the road and the border of houses to the west was unusually dark. I still hate to think about what we could have encountered in such a place! Especially late at night.

Jake and I used a concrete bridge to cross the ditch and get farther away from dog-filled yards on the hillside above us. We received a good deal of noise for our passage, nonetheless.

The roadway bridge that we walked under at Golden Avenue was remarkable that night—brooding and spooky. There was a streetlight above, which created a stark contrast of light and shadow in the contours of its old architecture. It looked like something from another, less gentle time, to be admired, but avoided. Jake mentioned that it would be too easy to imagine a sentinel spirit peering down at us from above. Being watched by *anything* wasn't a very appealing idea at that moment!

After passing under the bridge, we were in a section of field I had remembered from my elementary school days as especially removed from surrounding suburbia. Thanks to the ditch and steep hills on both sides topped with an unbroken line of fencing, there were only two directions to go: north, perhaps a hundred yards to Imperial Highway, or back to Golden Avenue, which seemed like three times that distance from where we now stood. Not a good place to be discovered with ill-gotten goods! Escape could involve a climb—a mad scramble Jake couldn't muster.

Jake was rattling on about his dog, Pepper, biting the meter man or some silly thing when I stopped our advance to tell him my intentions.

"Okay, Jake, just above here is that other pumpkin stand."

I pointed to the incline on the other side of the ditch.

"We just go up this bank and down a little ways. You can wait nearby if you want to."

The bank I mentioned was monstrous as banks in the area went. I felt like a mountaineer while ascending its smooth clay contours. At the top was a barren field. It stretched for perhaps another hundred yards, parallel to Imperial Highway, then ended in avocado trees that surrounded a lone house. Just beyond was the pumpkin lot.

Another brief walk and we came upon the avocado trees. Jake hastily retreated into them to hide from traffic on the highway. Fearing that the often-clumsy Jake might trip over a sprinkler or loudly rustle dry leaves while walking, I told him to wait on the grove's outskirts. He gladly obliged.

I knew he wasn't about to have a change of heart and go with me, especially now… this was going to be more hairball than my last snag. I had carefully scanned this particular lot every time I passed it in my heap. It was familiar. Familiar because l had already contemplated its weak points with the hope I would do exactly what I was now about to attempt. I knew how to get beyond the fancy fencing of this stand. That wasn't a problem. However, there were a lot of bright lights directed on the ground where the pumpkins lay, and the lot was only yards away from two heavily traveled roads. It looked sketchy.

Leaving Jake behind with a bold march, I followed a dirt pathway to the edge of the fenced lot. There were several strands of barbed wire on the bottom eighteen inches of the fence, the rest being an impenetrable chick-wire. Without regard to the lights, but mindful of nearby traffic, I fell on my belly near the fence.

"Whoosh! Whiz!" Cars swept through the intersection at my feet. Luckily, I was at a slightly higher elevation than the street. By lying prone, I made it difficult for anyone to see me as they drove past. With a Marine crawl, I wiggled between the taught barbed wire with just a few minor penetrations of my jacket and jeans. I was inside. I looked at the trailer that guarded its orange flock. There was not a sound, movement, or light from inside.

I remembered what both Virge and Jake had told me of the people who run this stand every year. One of their assertions kept flashing to mind.

"They've got dogs. Big dogs. One's a Doberman, I think."

No dogs yet, only cedar poles. Tall ones with lights. Virge and Jake were mistaken. Everything was still.

The pumpkins on this lot were big! On a table just outside the trailer were enormous ones, larger than I could reach around with my arms. But I didn't have the nerve to sneak over there and carry such a huge burden away with me. I had only to crawl a few feet to put my hands on quite a few large perfectly shaped specimens.

Grabbing the pumpkin of my choice, I turned to the fence with a squirm and lifted the barbed wire. The pumpkin rolled neatly outside. I did the same with another; these would be enough. Sure, there were bigger ones around, but they'd be too much of a hassle to carry. Getting back out was easy.

"Wow!" Jake whisper-shrieked on seeing the two large pumpkins I carried. "Those are GREAT!"

"You carry one! They're heavy!" I groaned.

Going back down the steep bank at the drainage ditch with the two dead weights seemed formidable, so Jake and I carried our burdens across the ridge with the long stretch of fencing to Golden Avenue. We descended back to the drainage ditch easement at the old bridge. Trying to jockey my pumpkin onto my shoulder, I almost dropped it. I was lucky to have caught it after a sudden juggle. The pumpkins were so heavy and hard to hold that we frequently stopped to rest.

Dogs barked maliciously on all sides as we traveled the ravine. Jake and I stopped to hurl rocks at one unusually vicious cur, which was running loose. It retreated up the bank.

Our return home came late—around two in the morning. But, what a challenge I had overcome! And, I was elated! I was appreciative of the unfettered romp that night, and I was glad that my evil-doing remained within safe bounds. I think Jake was hoping I would bring pot, but who needed it? I was high on the October air.

At 8:30 the next morning, Jake and I met again. We were both exhausted. Jake had a school book under one arm. I presumed this gave him the proper school-going appearance when he left his house. He stated that his call to Yorba Linda Middle School posing as his father was a success, so we waited patiently in our smoke-out spot in The Field for Virge to leave the house. We soon changed our location to the Filipos' grove.

To keep his hooky secret, Jake had to wait until Virge left for class. He expected his brother to leave between 9:00 and 9:30 that morning. At 10:00, the old car that Virge used was still in the driveway. Jake cursed his sibling for making him wait. I too was so impatient to get into the house and finish Virge's and my secret Halloween costumes that I finally banged on the door and confronted Virge.

"I've come to finish the costumes," I told him.

"Yeah! You took work off today, right?" he inquired.

"Uh huh," I confirmed. "Are you going to have to leave for class this morning?"

"Yeah, I'm due there now," Virge said.

"Well, don't let me stop you. I'll just set up and get these things finished."

I held up a bag of black material for his inspection and then started to set up, only to find Virge following me around. He said he wanted to help.

"Aren't you going to class?" I asked.

"Nah, I'm skipping philosophy. I'll go to the next class at 11:15."

I was dismayed. Poor Jake. The first chance I had, I went out to the two-story tool shed in Virge's backyard—known among the Farises as "The Space House"—where Jake was now hiding. He must have thought the day ruined when I told him Virge hadn't left yet. He was agitated. I extracted additional materials for the secret costumes that were hidden, like Jake, in the shed's upper portion. The Space House was just across the chain-link fence from the Filipos' place, and I didn't want Midge to know I hadn't gone to work. She could easily have seen me if she'd been about, so I was wary as I descended the ladder with my additional supplies.

Virge was not much help to my costume building, and he eventually left for class. Jake, weary and fuming, came into the empty house after hearing my long awaited "He's gone." The rest of the day was uneventful, except for finishing the special costumes, which were part of a new prank that Virge and I both thought would be hilarious.

I had designed witch costumes that would allow us to shrink back down to trick-or-treating size! I made two hoop skirts by constructing concentric sets of coat-hanger-wire circles, and cutting and sewing together eighteen black tapered cloth gores for each skirt. I suspended the hoops in the parachute-like skirts with loops of thread. These costumes were for a double-whammy joke. The costumes' purpose was to give people the impression that we were children—little girls as witches. Squatting, with our long legs beneath our skirts, we would imitate little children and trick-or-treat. On receiving candy at someone's doorstep, we would leap up to our full height, and run off cackling a deep bass "Thank you!"

Virge returned late that afternoon and was excited that I had finished the costumes. Virge, his parents, and Midge for that matter, didn't think anything was unusual when Jake and I were seen at the usual times that day. But, in addition to seeing the finished skirts, Virge saw one of the big "Imperial Highway" pumpkins awaiting its face on top of the TV.

"Where'd you get that?!" he squealed.

I explained to him that Jake and I had gone on a big pumpkin-lot snatch, and he seemed to appreciate our achievement. He didn't admonish Jake as I had earlier thought he might, which was nice of him.

"Feel how heavy, Virge!" I insisted.

Virge took the pumpkin from me.

"Ah!" he cried. "It's heavy! Let's weigh it!"

It came to almost forty pounds on the dubiously accurate bathroom scale. I had earlier estimated it to be around thirty pounds. We weighed all our other pumpkins, too. The Big Max "volunteer" from the bike trail field was a whopping thirty-six pounds by this scale!

We carved fanciful faces in our trove of pumpkins that afternoon. I tried to enjoy the task, but my knife-mates were testy, particularly Virge, who insisted that the Big Max from the field be spared my blade for him. I ended up drawing the face, though. We perched this jack-o-lantern on the chimney with a blinking red Christmas bulb inside, which was a favorite thing for Virge, who had done the same with another large pumpkin two Halloweens earlier. Nice effect.

The author and the Big Max pumpkin
on the Faris residence roof

That evening, Virge and Jake and I went trick-or-treating again, this time hoping to get great reactions from everyone who saw our costumes. Beside the hoop skirts, the witch garbs consisted of a goofy paper-mâché airbrushed mask with a cheap cotton wig, a conical hat, vinyl cape, and, of course, the concealing skirts. Jake was an "old man" again, but this time he wore a more realistic mask (one I had swiped from the nearby Skaggs drugstore—a store affectionately known among us shoplifters as "Snaggs"). He also had a hat, overcoat, and walking stick. Freddy was off with the Troy High School Band somewhere.

Verge and I dressed in Freddy's and my room. Our first stop was Verge's place, where we received candy from his father. As instructed, Jake snapped a photo of his dad's surprised mug on opening the front door. Because he wasn't aware of our costume project, Mr. Faris thought we were small children! After getting our candy, we squealed childlike thank-you's and waddled away with some pain, scrunched beneath the skirts. We then went to neighboring homes.

We limited our joke to Verge's Street. Although we received more good reactions to our joke than bad, Verge soon worked himself into yet another snit over the hot costume and the few put-off, fuddy-duddy candy givers we encountered. I enjoyed the laughter and shock we gave most of the people, but did agree that the damnable "Aren't you a little old for this kind of thing?" questions were annoying. I guess they didn't get the joke.

At one point, Verge flounced off in a fiery tither, cursing the costume I had slaved over for him. He ripped the upper portions from his body, never to don them again. Luckily, Jake had snapped a photo of us with his instamatic* earlier, just after we had more happily pursued trying to scare the neighbor girl next door. After Verge left the scene, a nasty teen girl unmasked me, and I lost my hat, only to find it later in the gutter. I had had enough, too.

I watched the Big Max pumpkin sitting on the Faris' chimney blink its demonic face. My mood had darkened. Mr. Faris' claim that he didn't know the identity of the witches did little to raise my spirits, though everyone had a good laugh on seeing us out front, unmasked, in the hoop skirts.

At this point, I thought a terrifying costume would put a kick into the evening. Jake and I went back to the Filipos' where I slipped into my more frightening Plexiglas "black knight" armor and skeleton warrior mask. Virge had gone elsewhere in disgust, so Jake and I walked down the bike trail, hoping to scare some younger kids.

I only caught glimpses of far-off trick-or-treaters. Colorful specks were moving from shadow to light and then quickly into shadow again. Parents conversed somewhere in the distance. There was the faint giggle of wide-eyed goblins encountering each other.

The "little witches." Virge Faris is on the left and the author is on the right. We're looking through the nostrils of the masks.

One of the Imperial Highway pumpkin stand's pumpkins, carved (standard 12oz. soda can shown for size)

Damn! Now, *I* was hot and sweaty and bored. I was disappointed in the whole evening. All the delicious stuff had already happened that month. This Halloween was stale.

I craved the sound of a bursting pumpkin! Going back to Freddy's grove in growing anger, I threshed the shrubs for the two small pumpkins Jake and I had gotten from the Boy Scout stand the previous night. We hadn't bothered to carve these little ones, and we hid them because a suspicious number of pumpkins might bring parental inquiries. I quickly found them and the destructive fun I had two years earlier came speeding back from the void.

"Crowlp! Plomp!"

The seed-filled fruits exploded on Rose Drive. Jake laughed gleefully.

"Where's the big one?" I snorted.

I loudly extracted a big uncarved pumpkin from the lot on Imperial Highway from the brush, then hurled it onto the street with a grunt. It landed close to a speeding car, but the driver seemed indifferent to the projectile exploding all over the pavement. I leaped into the road and crushed the larger pieces with well-placed stomps of my steel-toed boots. Jake crowed, practically in hysterics. This Halloween was now officially over, and a rotten one it had been, too.

The next morning, Jake and I took turns photographing each other with our carved pumpkins. I wanted photos because some were an impressive size. Proof also of what Virge and Freddy had at one time called the "impossible snatch." Impossible? Such a thought could only raise my dampened spirits. ◼

· CHAPTER 11 ·

MY AFFAIR WITH THE PINK LADY OF YORBA LINDA

 I have fond memories of the fall I spent in residence with the Filipos in Yorba Linda. I had been rooming with Freddy since the previous April, and our consequential escapades had already become too numerous to recall. The new fall season held promise for even greater undoings. It was late September 1980, and with the first brisk autumn air that foretold an end to the sultry summer, my thoughts turned to past Halloweens romping around in the cool twilight, kicking up the fallen leaves, costumes, parties, tricks and treats.

Ah, yes. Tricks! Forget the treats! I've always loved pranks, and the more they verged on a full-blown hoax—the more confusion and fear they created—the more I liked them. I wanted this Halloween to be a real blow-out—something genuinely memorable, outshining all the rest. I knew that with Freddy's ingenuity and my creative talents anything was possible. And, as it would turn out, I wouldn't be disappointed.

It all started at Volt Technical Corporation, where I worked as a display ad artist at a drawing board. Virge had taken to calling me "money bags" because I was out of high school, worked forty hours a week, and made five dollars an hour. (This is the equivalent of $15.38 an hour at the time of this writing.) The minimum wage was $3.10 an hour in 1980, and Virge worked only part-time at a Marie Callender's as a cook making minimum wage. So, the "money bags" moniker was a bit of an exaggeration and a little annoying.

I was sitting in my little Volt cubicle one lunchtime, thumbing through a few books, when along came my diminutive coworker, Pete Scalzo. He approached me with his eyes on high beam.

"Ghosts!" he exclaimed. "Where'd you get these?"

"Just books from the Yorba Linda Library," I said, trying to look bored.

"Any good?" Pete inquired.

"Really good!" I retorted, pushing one of parapsychologist Hans Holzer's* remarkable "true account" editions under his nose.

Pete was sometimes indignant about his lot in life. He saw himself as an impoverished artist who was wasting his talents at Volt. He was also sure that his Volt supervisors were plotting to make his existence miserable, and that there was no God. Otherwise, he was generally quiet and unassuming. He did have a reputation at Volt for a short temper and a bad attitude, though. He also saw himself as some kind of Casanova and bothered certain lady co-workers, which led to run-ins with supervisors and the more gallant males in the department.

Pete was a twenty-four-year-old of both Japanese and Italian heritage with a moon-pie face sporting glasses. His black Prince Valiant hair receded from a billboard of a forehead. I got to know Pete the previous spring when I first started work at Volt. We both drew cartoons when our supervisors weren't around, sniggering at our creations. We also made toys out of our tape and drafting equipment while we should have been working. We seemed to share the same interests and immaturities, so we got along fine. However, when it came to our religio-philosophical beliefs, we couldn't see eye to eye.

Not wholly convinced that Christianity had all the answers, it still had some appeal for me at the time. But, I was plagued by logic, and faith just didn't seem enough. The sudden realization of my mortality at the age of eighteen had driven me to indulge in literature on all sorts of esoteric subjects—psychic phenomena, the supernatural—things people could see or experience that might point to other dimensions or even an afterlife.

Pete was a closed-minded atheist who threw up a formidable barrier against my church-school offerings, but this reading material I had… ghosts intrigued him!

I believe in ghosts—hell, lots of people do! Pete had already told me about his friend in Upland who lived in a "haunted house." He must have believed that there were "atmospheric conditions" that replay "place memories" or some such thing, if not in an afterlife. So began the gears, the mighty cogs in my mind. A hoax, a grand hoax! The unforgettable October!

"Have you ever heard of the 'Pink Lady' of Yorba Linda?" I asked Pete one morning at work.

"No, I don't believe I have," he replied skeptically.

"Well," I began, "the Pink Lady is a ghost reportedly seen many times in the Yorba Historical Cemetery. It's supposed to be an annual thing—like she's seen roaming around on a particular night in October or something."

Pete squinted.

"Really?"

"Sure!" I said, turning to look across the art department. "Karen or Sarah have probably heard about the ghost—it's famous! Ask them about it at break."

What I said was true. Since I was a mere skiod, I had heard stories about a pink phantom that roamed an old Spanish graveyard in eastern Yorba Linda. Once, in the fourth grade, I went to the place to end my curiosity, and even during the day and with other kids, it was a scary place—way off the road, big tombstones, twisted trees, the whole bit. I hadn't visited it since.

Sarah and Karen were attractive girls two cubicles over, who lived in Placentia and Yorba Linda, respectively. Karen was slightly surprised when the question popped out of Pete's mouth; she never talked to him much. Then came an answer that would further my cause.

"Yeaaaah… I've heard of it. My husband and I went there in June when it's supposed to appear. There were a bunch of high school kids in the graveyard. One guy was running around in a sheet, trying to scare everybody."

Pete's jaw dropped so violently I was sure he had jarred a few teeth loose.

"Really?" he exclaimed. "So it's well known!"

Sarah had heard of it. Gerry had heard of it, too. My God, yes! It was well known! Half a dozen people confirmed that they had either heard of the legend or had actually gone to the cemetery to check it out. There was also an article in the October 1980 issue of *Orange Coast Magazine* that told about the hundreds of people who put up lawn chairs around the graveyard and waited to see it—rock music blaring from ghetto blasters, empty beer cans flying from the hands of those with even less respect. Throngs go there on a specific night in June, hoping to see the phantom in her flowing pink gown. It's supposed to be a fucking circus.

With the Volt consensus, Pete's interest in ghosts grew tenfold, and he and I spent more time together. Eventually, he became the perfect pigeon for a great joke. I suggested we visit the Yorba Cemetery one night soon and Pete was ready.

TALL TALES

"My friend Virgil Faris and I have seen it," I lied to Pete in confidence. "We went to the graveyard late one June night… I can't remember what time… but we saw it, and it was really pink! God, I thought I'd piss my pants! We ran like hell!"

Pete's eyes grew ever wider.

"Virge must be sensitive to this kind of thing," I continued, "you know, ESP. But I don't think I have powers. The ghost is real. I know it is. It looked right at us, and man were we close! We were drunk, too. I think that's why we ran."

And so I wove the tangled web. The tall tale had various details that Pete might have called me on if he saw a discrepancy in any retelling, but for the eventual perfection of my plan, they would all prove advantageous. I just had to remember them all. Pete still didn't believe in ghosts, but with my story, his curiosity was beginning to get the best of him.

I saw Virge that afternoon at his house. He was more than willing to participate in a hoax. As I laid out more of the details of what I had already told Pete, his gears started to spin, too.

Freddy came in and fell lazily onto the Faris' old black vinyl couch.

"Freddy," Virge began with an unrestrained lilt in his voice, "Slade has a guy at work that he's set up for a big joke!"

"What kind of joke?" Freddy asked dubiously, trying vainly to spin Virge's basketball on his finger.

"Actually, it's more of a hoax… if we can pull it off," I said. "There's this joker at work—Pete Scalzo—I've been setting him up all this week for a prime ghost scare at the old Yorba Cemetery."

"I thought you said his name was 'Pete Spoo,'" Virge interrupted.

"No!" I said. "That's a cartoon-strip character he modeled after himself! Anyway, this guy thinks he knows it all. He's a great target."

I gave Freddy more details of the incredible tale I related to Pete, Pete's intense interest, etcetera. A smile began to form parallel to his curly red Abe Lincoln beard. Soon, Virge and Freddy were both getting as excited about the prank as I was.

Now, all we needed was the ghost. That was the big problem. It would be a woman's ghost, pink even, but the task of making something like a dummy or painting appear and disappear seemed phenomenally difficult. I knew all along that Virge and Freddy would go for a good scare, and fears of having to pull off a stunt by myself never surfaced once. Our minds thrummed in deep thought. A cog slipped.

"How about a smoke bomb with a Pink-Lady-shaped light shining on the smoke screen?" I offered.

The absurdity of my suggestion was immediately thrown back into my face by Virge.

"No!" he said adamantly. "How anyone could see a likeness of a woman in smoke… it's stupid!"

"Yeah," chimed Freddy. "Why not just a basketball on a fishing line, covered with a sheet, like in that *Brady Bunch* episode?"

"No!" I roared, not appreciating the sarcasm.

"A painting on cardboard, cut to the proper shape might do it!" Freddy countered. "We could hide it in the hedge and stick it up through the top using a pole and shine a flashlight on it!"

"Naw, that's too two-dimensional," I groaned. "It'd never work."

"Lasers!" Virge burst out. "Edmund Scientific catalog has laser hologra…"

He was stopped short reaching for the catalog by our exasperated gazes.

"No, no, no!" Freddy and I crowed.

The troubleshooting for this hoax was going to be as tricky as some of our other ideas that never saw light: a humongous tissue-paper hot-air balloon dick and balls—airbrushed to life-like perfection and crowned with brown tinsel pubic hair—launched to defile the airspace of Yorba Linda (along with a matching set of giant breasts)… Black-shrouded, gourd-head aliens with glowing eyes invading the bike trail… Tunnels to stash our ill-gotten goods… Kinetic sculptures we could ride like bikes. Bah!

We all became steeped in thought again, and after a few moments, Freddy's platinum-blond head snapped up.

"How about a painting on screen?"

"Hmmm, sounds like it might work," I said.

"Yeah!" Virge rang out. "Yeah! Shine a flashlight on it!"

Sheer brilliance!

Virge suggested that we use his sliding back door screen and even proceeded to remove it, but Freddy and I assured him that it wasn't necessary to chance his father's fury. On September 22, I went to Builders' Emporium in Fullerton after work and bought eight feet of plastic door screen.

BULLSHIT MACHINE

I told Virge the intricate story I had related to Pete. He would confirm it to Pete on the night of the scare to keep everything sounding kosher. Virge was to pretend to be twenty-two, rather than seventeen, as we thought Pete might take him more seriously if he were an older chap. Virge was to tell Pete that he had "out of the ordinary" experiences to add a spooky ESP guy to the mix. Coupled with the "facts" of my ghost-sighting story re-uttered by Virge, we hoped Pete would be convinced that I had been telling the truth at work all along.

Pete was already considering that if there was a ghost, Virge, or both Virge and I, were psychic, which led to some deliberation at work between Pete and me.

There was some essential bullshit Pete was to believe for the successful completion of the scare. We told him that security guards were patrolling the cemetery area at night, keeping a lookout for vandals. We wanted our setup, whatever it was to be, to be quiet and inconspicuous. Nearby residents alerting the police to "vandals" in the confines of the graveyard was a concern. If Pete were wary of guards, he'd be extra careful to be quiet. A condominium community bordering the cemetery Virge had told me about was a likely place for guards, so we were to tell Pete they came from there.

"If we create too much noise," I'd tell Pete at work, "we'd surely be asked to leave. Three or four people is as many as we can risk taking in quietly and safely at one time."

Actually, of even greater concern than the police was attracting people in general. Someone might detect the fake ghost rig, which was something we couldn't chance. So, we were all to be very quiet, especially Pete, who had no real experience sneaking silently about like we did.

From what Virge had told me, people were now in great abundance around the cemetery. It was no longer the eerie little pepper tree and oleander lined burial ground set back from the road and alone in a field. After major earth moving, it now sat on a hilltop surrounded by residential streets and hundreds of tract homes and condos. We had to be careful.

Also, I had said Virge and I saw the ghost off in a field on the east side of the cemetery during a drunken dare in 1978. Luckily, Pete didn't find out that the houses around it, and in said field, had been there since 1976. The facts wouldn't have fit together!

Virge and Freddy had both been to the Yorba Cemetery after school football games. They went there with friends several times in the past and knew what it was like now. I hadn't been since I was a grade-schooler, but later that week in September we'd all go out there to case the joint.

After work, I'd busy myself with creating the spirit, and everything seemed to be coming together. At Volt, I continued to string Pete along. Soon, he was so excited about going to the cemetery that I set a date… that Sunday night, October 5. I chose Sunday night thinking most of the locals would be asleep early. No people around meant no hassles for our set up. Pete agreed to the time, assuming the "guards" would be less of a problem on such a quiet night.

Virge and Freddy would have to drive to the graveyard separately of Pete and me for the stunt to work. Pete had heard enough about Virge to want him along on our "ghost watch." Pete was cool with driving, too, so long as I could direct him to the graveyard.

During all of this planning for the "scare"—which took place over the edge of Pete's cubicle in the form of little notes—another coworker of mine, Steve Sabine, whom I had sorely filled in on the hoax, expressed to me that he would like to join our ranks. I drew the pre-scare cartoon on the next page, with Steve shown on the right of our group in the YWCA sweatshirt. Also shown in the group, from left to right, is me, Virge and Pete.

Steve had a strange, quirky sense of humor. Among other things, he once stated that he would like to have a rabbi sit on his feet and eat pork. He also wanted to attend Volt's annual Halloween luncheon dressed as a wedge or some other basic shape. I included Steve in the poster art I created for the event (also on the next page).

The combination of Steve's flip remarks, swish-walking, limp-wristed voice, and punk-rock hairdo gave many conservative menfolk an uneasy feeling. And, Pete, in addition to being a failed womanizer, was a bit of a homophobe. Steve couldn't abide this in the slightest and considered Pete a creep at best. If one could overlook Steve's strong anti-establishment attitudes and fruity appearance, his acting talents were apparent. He could, as he put it, "give a terrified scream and crumple to the ground in a dead faint," which sounded good to me. The prospect of a piercing feminine shriek at the sight of our ghost just couldn't be denied. We needed a great emotional needler, and up until that point, I would have done all the screaming—something terribly undignified. Steve wanted to scare Pete, and scare Pete badly, so he was "in."

the Halloween Luncheon.

I told Pete that Steve was going along to the cemetery with us, and Pete was immediately apprehensive. I was not aware that Steve's animosity for Pete had become mutual. However, Pete was determined to see the graveyard and its ghost, even if he had to suffer through Steve's typical non-stop sarcastic commentary.

The event was now essentially set. I was to get in contact with Pete and Steve early that weekend of the 5th and give them the times it would be most suitable to go, Virge supposedly working and having to drive there "alone." Now it was time to move on our rig.

THE "MISSUS" AND THE PLAN

During the week of September 19–26, I worked on the creation that would come to be known as "The Missus." Little did I realize the potential of this new screen painting idea at the outset. In the Filipos' garage, I laid down one of the cardboard voting booths we had stolen from a supply room at Rose Drive Elementary School early the previous summer. On one side, I drew the outline of a woman—actually three-quarters of a woman—her legs fading off into nothing. I then sketched in some features: long hair, a ruffed collar, and a strange circular sash. I knew nothing about old Spanish clothing, especially the length of skirts (and didn't take time to research it), but this didn't seem essential.

The first drawing I made was too large. If it were a life-size representation of a real woman, she would have been of monstrous proportions. I flipped the cardboard over and started again. The next drawing was better, shapelier, even sexy. Perfect! I placed about five feet of screen over the drawing, taped it down, and stood it up for painting.

Mixing some red and white tempera paint (also from Rose Drive Elementary), I proceeded to paint the screen with my airbrush. The figure was a definite pink, with stark black and white overtones. She had no eyes, just dark sockets under tresses of flowing black hair. The rectangular screen background was also black. She still had no legs, but was definitely a woman—a masterpiece of evil intent! We even had an additional full painting on the cardboard backer where the paint went through the holes in the screen—a pink twin sister!

For a week, The Missus hung in the garage or the empty bedroom Freddy's sister had recently vacated. It was suspended on black thread, with a black metal antenna hanger to spread the screen. Many times, Freddy or I would enter the dimly lit room forgetting our ghost was there and have our heart stop at the glimpse of it. The effect was incredible! The light-colored figure stood out in bold relief with the slightest amount of light, while the black screen, metal hanger, and supporting thread remained invisible. It looked almost three-dimensional!

Cartoons Pete drew depicting our anticipated ghost watch (pages 142 and 143) became more hilarious by the minute now that our spirit posed such a threat to the skepticism they depicted.

The airbrushed ghost, "The Missus"

One evening that week, Virge and Freddy and I tested The Missus by hanging her in the huge Canary Island Pine at the top of the driveway. We had already experimented with tubes and funnels on a flashlight to direct the light in a controllable, constricted field. But, after each of us had run down the hill to different positions, and had viewed the apparition with various illuminations filtered with our fingers, the modifications to the light beam proved unreliable. It was also apparent that there could be no foliage behind the screen image, as the needles of the pine also manifested in the flashlight beam. Ideally, we needed a patch of unobstructed sky beneath a tree.

We then began to question the plausibility of pulling off this feat with the limited number of trees around the graveyard. We required long, outstretched limbs with very few leaves. Not having seen the cemetery for many years, and before all the homes had sprouted up, I imagined Freddy out in an expansive field, clustered with his equipment in the weeds under a lone tree. As it would turn out, I was to find the new surroundings seriously more suburban, but with more trees than expected.

"We've got to have a tree alone, against the bare sky," I told Freddy.

"Yeah, but it'll be hard to find one with a branch sticking out enough to hang the ghost," he muttered.

"We'll have to see about that when we case the graveyard," Virge added impatiently.

Virge was right. It would soon be necessary to survey the cemetery during daylight hours to work out the mechanics of the stunt. The set up wouldn't be difficult once we found an appropriate tree—*if* we could find one!

Despite our first complex and unrealistic thoughts on this hoax, we were wise enough to use a simple, easy-to-use form of ghost. In addition to "The Missus," we referred to the painting as either a "screen painting" or the unrelated term, "hologram," which indicated its three-dimensional quality. The ghost was to be operated solely by Freddy, who would sit behind a hedge or bush, completely hidden from our view. At a specified time, he would raise the screen by pulling on an invisible fishing line. The monofilament fishing line was to be looped over a long, lateral limb with the screen weighted by large metal nuts. The nuts were attached to a specific measure of black thread and would stop the screen at an appropriate height (they were also intended to keep the wind from blowing the image around). Freddy would then shine his lantern on the image for approximately a minute, moving his fingers across the flashlight lens to make the ghost appear and again to make it disappear. After making The Missus evaporate, Freddy would release his pull line and scurry quietly away with the whole rig. Virge's car was to be nearby, but opposite the graveyard from where I would make Pete park. Freddy would get in Virge's car and drive home with Virge.

Neat, clean, simple—just as long as we could set it up without people catching us! As for the roles the rest of us would play, Virge was to act "spacey," indicating his "ESP." Steve was to scream, wet his pants, or do whatever he deemed necessary to add to the excitement once the ghost appeared. I was to act suitably frightened. Nothing over the top.

These shenanigans were all with Pete in mind, of course. I had never more than startled someone with a prank, so this would be interesting.

A little explanation may be needed here: Pink Lady was a massively popular music duo in Japan during the early 1980s. They even had a musical hit here in America, as well as a short-lived TV show in the U.S. entitled, "Pink Lady and Jeff." Mie and Kei, the Japanese members of Pink Lady, didn't speak a lick of English. They not only spoke their television parts in English by rote, but also sang every song that way as well. The show now ranks #35 on TV Guide's list of "The 50 Worst TV Shows of All Time."[2] "Oh shit!" Indeed.

I had a twist on Pete's skepticism, too. Just what would it take to create a successful hoax? Virge's crazy lasers? All of these cartoons were drawn while we should have been performing our jobs at Volt.

The entrance to the Yorba Historical Cemetery as it appeared in 1981

YORBA HISTORICAL CEMETERY

I couldn't believe my eyes the morning Virge and I drove into the area that I last remembered as an enormous rolling field of wild grasses. We were on our way to the cemetery to do some initial reconnaissance for the hoax.

"This place has changed so much!" I said in awe of the labyrinth of streets and houses. "Where's the graveyard?"

"Tum right!" Virge squawked. "You blew it! Now we'll have to go around!"

It wasn't anything like I remembered from my childhood. I guess that's Southern California for you! Houses, condos, and apartments had popped up like mushrooms after a rain.

This is how I remembered the Yorba Historical Cemetery. The hill in the background shows that housing developments were already encroaching on the area by the late sixties (1969 photo courtesy Orange County Archives).

We circled a large block of condominiums.

"Here!" Virge pointed. "Stop here."

I pulled over, across the street from more condos and a stone's throw from several racquetball courts.

"So *there's* the graveyard," I groaned, bemoaning the intrusions of all the cookie-cutter neighborhoods.

Virge and I walked up a tidy little white sidewalk past some aspen-like trees where there once had been a dirt footpath. We walked past street lights, lawns, neat plantings, sprinklers, path lamps. So, this was what it was like now! Not so bad really. The cemetery itself was basically the same. Age-old California peppers still loomed over the poor man's wood cross and the rich men's marble monoliths. Crumbling crypts, poking up like concrete curbing, snaked through lush clusters of mondo grass.

Virge had told me there were also depressions in the soil that snatched an unwary foot like a zombie's hand. A friend of Virge fell victim to these and was lucky not to have sprained an ankle. Virge and his school chums used to come here after high school football games to feel a little haunted. Some added beer drinking, smoking dope, and vandalizing the headstones to the experience.

Founding father Bernardo Yorba's stone, a massive squarish thing, was still intact though, untouched by time as well as vandals. A marker at a new entrance just as silently displayed the family name, "Yorba Historical Cemetery, Established 1858." The metal trellis-tunnel entrance was new, like the surrounding wrought iron fence and low hedge that had replaced the oleander bushes I had remembered. But, everything else looked as old as the bones here.

Through the entry were concrete paving stones to accommodate our light footfall.

"Shit!" I said, peeved by a pile of beer cans and broken bottles.

"What? Oh yeah," Virge replied, glancing at the debris. "They come here after the games."

The disrespect of my contemporaries disgusted me. I hated that.

I tiptoed among the graves while taking in the grandeur of two tall junipers that swept into the sky. Then, Virge called my attention to a gravestone beneath a pepper tree and near a pink oleander.

The Anna Fuentez tombstone

"I think this is the 'Pink Lady!'" he said, pointing to a small upright stone.

It belonged to a Spanish woman, Anna Fuentes, who died as a teenager sixty-three years before either of us had been born.

"Really?" I asked.

"I think so," Virge replied, squatting, as I was, next to the stone like a gargantuan sprite.

"We'll have to show this to Pete!" I piped.

For all practical purposes, Ms. Fuentes was the Pink Lady. That is, up until we read after the hoax that she was not the donor of the local spirit. Most sources say that the Pink Lady is Alvina de los Reyes, a descendant of the Yorba family and that she was killed in a buggy accident while returning from a dance at Valencia High School.[3] Another source, "psychic artist" Barbara Soblewski, visited the cemetery and got impressions that the ghost was a woman named Ellie Castillo.[4] We also read that the spirit was rumored to be seen only in even-numbered years, and only on June 15. She walks among the graves, kneels, weeps, and then fades away. Pretty romantic stuff. Anyway, Anna Fuentes was the specter for our purposes. Pete didn't research it, so we were fine.

Virge showed me an opening in the south hedge which we squeezed through with some effort and noise. There were a remarkable number of planted trees and shrubs just outside of the cemetery. Most made a heavy, useful blind from the west and south. It was virtually impossible to know there was anything like the graveyard on the hilltop by looking from the streets. On the north side, there was a tennis court only a few yards from the entrance gates, as well as sycamore trees, a drinking fountain, sand pits with see-saws and jungle gyms, and a ball-field-size lawn at the foot of some reasonably far-off homes on another hillside. It was a full-fledged park. To the east, there was more lawn and more condos—the condos we'd tell Pete included guards.

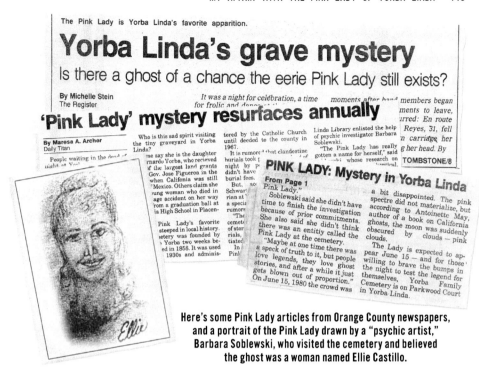

The Pink Lady is Yorba Linda's favorite apparition.

Yorba Linda's grave mystery

Is there a ghost of a chance the eerie Pink Lady still exists?

By Michelle Stein
The Register

'Pink Lady' mystery resurfaces annually

By Maresa A. Archer
Daily Titan

PINK LADY: Mystery in Yorba Linda

Here's some Pink Lady articles from Orange County newspapers, and a portrait of the Pink Lady drawn by a "psychic artist," Barbara Soblewski, who visited the cemetery and believed the ghost was a woman named Ellie Castillo.

FRIDAY

Freddy, Virge and Jake Faris, and I were searching the park east of the graveyard for a suitable tree. The tree had to present our Missus clearly, but be discreet enough to hide her from late-night dog walkers and the like. We hadn't decided on one the day Virge and I had been there.

It was Friday night, and Freddy was anxiously scouting out trees with us, as the weekend of the scare was upon us. He ran up a succulent-covered bank too near a house.

"Rowf! Rowf! Rowf!"

A toothy red ball of fur threw itself against the fence near Freddy, who was clambering in and out of tree branches.

"C'mon, Freddy!" I urged. "There's not any good trees here after all!"

Virge egged Freddy further, and the thrashing of branches continued.

"ROWR-ROWR-ROWR!" The fur ball was whipped into a frenzied lather.

Jake and I walked off toward the cemetery in dismay. "This is incredibly assholish!" I grunted. "It's still light out, and they're going to have all kinds of people on their cases for crawling through their trees!"

The interior of the Yorba Historical Cemetery in 1980

Bernardo Yorba's gravestone and the inside of the cemetery entrance in the 80s

Jake agreed, to be polite. He still wasn't sure what we intended to prove by assaulting the local vegetation, though he knew the bare bones of our ghost hoax.

In the fading light, I could see Freddy's poorly camouflaged clothing flash in the underbrush on the hillside. A wisp of steam twined from my tightening lips in exasperation. "Let's go…" I said to myself.

A small dark figure appeared on the walkway of a nearby house directly above Freddy, who was now ascending the bank in plain view. Then, another character appeared. Virge, standing at the bottom of the bank, made several quick gestures with his lanky arms, and Freddy looked above him. He then descended to the field with a few quick hops. They soon rejoined us.

"None of those trees look very promising," I informed the two glum plant molesters. "The bank would show a lot of the light from the flashlight. And, besides, there's no place to hide Freddy."

"True," Virge agreed. "Maybe over there."

"Over there" was a point south-west of Virge's outstretched finger. It included the banks that separated the cemetery from the streets. There were fairly big trees there, but were they too close to where we'd stand in the graveyard to chance a shiny wire or a rustle of leaves? There were the sidewalks there too—a nighttime venue for joggers or other ghost seekers, no doubt.

Despite the abundance of trees on the south bank, few allowed a flashlight beam to clear their branches. We had a choice between two small eucalyptus, so we chose the one closest to the middle of the graveyard's south hedge. It was on the edge of a lawn and at the top of the ice-plant-covered bank. The hedge would conceal Freddy admirably, and shrubs on the bank would allow him to take refuge from passersby if need be.

Freddy stood, hands on hips, gazing at the tree.

"Yeah!" Virge squealed. "This tree is great!"

Freddy agreed. It was a great tree, an excellent tree—far enough away from street lights, open limbs to the sky. Everything except…

"Hmmm," Freddy reflected, lost in one of those deep Freddy thoughts we had all come to admire.

Before I knew it, he was scaling the tree with Virge close behind.

"These branches won't do," he told us.

"Damn!" I fumed. "They're sticking up too much?!"

"Yeah. Too upright," Freddy announced.

He scanned the elegant branches for another minute or so, but despite his Freddy-thought, he came down discouraged. Then there was a gleam in his big blue eyes.

"What we need…" he said thoughtfully, "is a fake branch!"

"A fake branch? Yes, a fake branch!" Virge and I cried. "Of course! But how?"

Freddy was quick to solve the problem facing us.

"We'll use a pole. We can camouflage it with eucalyptus branches and lash it to the tree!"

We'd do it. As ludicrous as it sounded, we all knew we'd do it! But, I still questioned our limited engineering abilities.

MIDGE, ARNIE, STEVE, PETE, AND THE BIG BRANCH

"Hello, lovely people!" Midge twittered to some fat guests who had just braved the long driveway to the Filipo's doorstep in their land yacht. Freddy and I looked at one another, silently interrupting our work with a silly "there-she-goes-again" smirk. Freddy's mother was only so sweet when outsiders came to call, or when a day was particularly good. She was more often cranky and bitchy. The play-acting she did for her guests seemed so artificial that it was funny. It was damned disappointing to see so much inherent nastiness sprung so often on Freddy, and not on some unsuspecting idiot. Those who had enough nerve to phone Midge during her rather intense musical studies at her piano were in danger of getting theirs though. She was choir director for St. Martin's Catholic Church, and one night the phone rang one too many times.

"Damn these people calling me all night!" Midge barked.

But, somehow, she swallowed the fire and brimstone on lifting the receiver.

"Ohhh, hiii!" she'd begin, saccharine-sweet. "Howww are you? Oh, I'm *sooo* glad!"

I suppose she had fine control.

Arnie, Freddy's father, was different. One might expect him to grunt "Gimme eat!" at the dinner table, but for his determined brow, shaven head, and other militaristic, somewhat barbaric properties, he was a well-mannered gentleman. Except, of course, when Freddy called him a "jerk" for demanding he hit his homework. Then, Arnie—or "Narnie" as we would sometimes affectionately call him behind his back—would throw a few kangaroo-like jabs, bruising Freddy's elbow or breaking his watch. Usually the latter, due to bad aim.

The proverbial sneak-out was the most significant risk in this hoax, and Arnie and Midge were not the type of parents who would just let us become as delinquent as we unnoticeably, but honestly were. Yes, we had been caught coming back in the house from a sneak-out, even stoned I'm sorry to say. Virge and Jake had also been apprehended by their nocturnally unpredictable "pee and em" on their exits or returns. But, for the most part, we snuck out undetected and were able to get the parents to buy some lame excuse on the couple of occasions when we were discovered. But how long could that last?

Like other times, both Arnie and Midge would need to be substantially asleep for the ghostly sneakings-out. What was more difficult was that Virge and Freddy would need to be setting up the "rig" when both their parents were still awake. Shortly after 11:00 on the next night was when they'd set it up, only minutes after normal parental bed-down. At least Virge had a history of working late and would have an excuse.

"Where are we going to tell Arnie and Midge we're going tonight?" Freddy inquired of me after Midge's visitors had waddled out of sight.

"Well, it's Saturday. We can tell them we're all going to Camelot to play miniature golf," I said, taping another branch of eucalyptus to an old pool pole supplied by Virge.

"Yeah, that's good enough," said Freddy. "We'll have to tell Virge when he gets home from work."

We were standing ankle-deep in clippings from the leafy, charitable sentinels of the bike trail that balmy afternoon. The pool pole was the primary support for our artificial limb, and after using up most of a roll of masking tape to apply a dozen or so small limbs to the pole, we successfully altered its straight appearance.

"This is a lot of work," I complained. "I hope that this thing looks like a real branch when we get it up in that tree. This paint doesn't look like a eucalyptus bark color."

"Yes, it does!" said Freddy, frowning. "Don't worry."

A dollop of light brown paint plopped on his Vans as I globbed a brush laden with tempera paint on the tape joints.

"Just paint everything… Uh, you missed a spot," Freddy said, pointing to some bare metal.

Suddenly, his face screwed up almost fitfully.

"I gotta go pinch a loaf," he announced. "I'll be right back."

And off he went.

Just then, Virge appeared on the raised ground between his backyard and Freddy's garage.

"How does it look?" I inquired, raising the unwieldy branch for his inspection.

"Okay," he muttered solemnly.

"Have a bad day at work?" I asked.

"Yeah, I'm tired."

Forewarned of his apparent lousy mood, I foolishly reminded him that we were going to lash up the limb that night. He proceeded to tell me he didn't want to go, and our conversation digressed into some rather personal bone-picking. When Freddy returned from the lavatory (a frequent sanctuary of his), he had better luck with Virge, and Virge left less perturbed. Luckily, a nap had refreshed Virge from his lousy day and equally miserable thoughts when next we met. Working as a cook at Marie Callender's in Placentia must have been shitty.

Arnie soon presented himself near our dirt-patch work area behind the garage, half smiling.

"What are you guys doing now?" he asked.

"Making props for Halloween!" we replied after some quick thinking.

"Oh… all right," he said. "You boys just make sure you clean up this mess before your mother sees it."

The lack of his usual concern for details relieved us, and he walked away. Midge was still busy entertaining her guests. I heard her guffaw inside—most likely at something only she found amusing.

The big branch was stashed away under orange trees in the grove for retrieval that night. As the day drew to a close, I phoned Steve Sabine from the privacy of Arnie and Midge's bedroom.

"Are you still coming?" I asked.

"Where?" was Steve's reply.

"To the graveyard to scare Pete!" I insisted.

"Oh, uh, no. I can't make it," Steve said matter-of-factly. "I had food poisoning from some old potato salad or something at a party last night. I was just at the doctor. I'm really not up to driving out there from Whittier."

Steve was one to stay out late drinking on weeknights. He sometimes awoke the next morning stretched across his car seat in some parking lot. Often the door was left open all night. It's incredible a near-sighted rapist hadn't violated him yet (but then maybe that was the idea). I assumed he was drunk, drinking, or going out to drink, if not already nursing a hangover, but I played along.

"Wow... I'm sorry you got that stuff. Pretty serious, huh?"

"Yes. Looks like you'll have to go without me."

"Well, okay," I sighed.

"Click!"

What a dick! Now I'd have to do all the screaming and needling! Shit. Oh well, I didn't want to be in his company if we were arrested for disturbing the peace, anyway.

I dialed Pete's number.

"Hello, Pete?"

"Yes?" buzzed the receiver.

"This is Slade. How are you?"

"Fine."

"Good... good. Are you still planning to go out to the graveyard with Virge and me tomorrow night?"

"Ah... it depends on what time you guys are going down there."

Fuck! The subject of our toil has second thoughts? First Virge, then Steve, now this dick! I overcame my initial surprise.

"Well, we figured we could meet at about 11:30, 11:45, around then. Virge has to work late, so he'll drive straight there. I'll go with you and show you the way there, like we talked about."

It ended up that Virge *was* working late, and our plans centered around his quitting time—10:15 p.m.

"Is Freddy going, too?" Pete asked.

The pencil I was fiddling with instantly stopped its spastic jumping.

"Uh, no..." I said, whispering. "Freddy snuck out to a party and was caught coming in late. Uh, it's not a good idea for him to risk sneaking out again. He said he's going to stay home. He didn't want to go anyway."

"Oh," said Pete.

"By the way, Steve can't make it. He's got food poisoning!"

"Really," Pete answered, indifferently. "I still don't see why you have to sneak out. It's not like they're *your* parents!"

"Oh," I said, beginning to have bigger-than-life flashes of us all being pummeled by burly Arnie on our return from the scare. "It keeps the household at peace when I don't break from my 'nice kid' mold and insist on a lot of late-night romps."

"Okay. 11:30?"

"Uh huh, and remember… you don't need a flashlight. We aren't taking any. Be at the bottom of Freddy's driveway on Rose Drive about ten minutes after 11:00…"

I heard paper rustling in the receiver and imagined Pete's index finger pushing up on the nose-piece of his glasses in frustration.

"Tell me how to get there again."

I proceeded to relate the whole set of complicated directions as I had already done at work. Then came Pete's "I'll be there," and a satisfying "click." Pete would have to drive into Yorba Linda from some far-off area of Fullerton. I suppose his concern for getting lost was justifiable.

Everything was "go." We had all our necessary equipment for the effects, all our stories lined up for Pete, and our transportation and plans put together for the simple execution of our hoax. After dinner that night, Freddy announced that he and I and Virge would be going to the miniature golf park in Anaheim called Camelot.

"It's almost nine o'clock," Arnie reminded us.

"We know," Freddy replied reassuringly. "We'll only be gone a little while."

"All right, be back soon!" Arnie said as he strained his eyes on a PBS TV show in front of him.

Freddy twisted comically from his stance at the TV room door, almost bumping into Virge and me, who were standing in the hallway, grinning.

"Let's go!" he said with his own detectable smile.

Virge had parked his family's station wagon just inside of the driveway at the bottom of Freddy's hill, and with a little hunting, the pole-branch was found and paraded into the back where The Missus and her cardboard support were laying. I piled in, and Virge and Freddy followed, Freddy with a tweak on the bill of his ever-present camouflage ball cap. Virge heralded our start to the cemetery with a fast turn out of the driveway and a raucous "Wheeee!" Evidently, he was feeling better than he had earlier that evening.

Soon we were at the cemetery. We turned onto a side street leading to the tennis courts, stopping at the west bank of the graveyard. We parked in the darkness under a tree there, which covered an opening between condos. There was no one to be seen near a car parked behind us, or near the homes. There was no one at the tennis courts or anywhere on the street for that matter, either. The only sound I could detect was the "tack! tack! tack!" of kamikaze insects hurling themselves at a nearby streetlight.

We exited the car only to be stopped short by the headlights of an approaching vehicle. It turned onto another street, so we proceeded to the back of Virge's station wagon, being careful not to make any noise. I was getting a little nervous, even though I had mostly banished the thoughts of running into someone who could ruin our hard work from my mind. With the back window of the station wagon rolled down, I hoisted the branch out, looked to the left, looked to the right, and seeing it was clear, began crossing the lane to the park on the other side. Freddy and Virge busied themselves with extracting the delicate Missus and her tangle of lines.

Suddenly, there was a flash of color down the street! I froze for just a second, then realizing my mistake, scurried up a slope to a grassy area on the north-west corner of the graveyard. Standing still, balancing the heavy pole and breathing ever harder, I looked down on a funny-looking loady* who whizzed past Virge and Freddy on his yellow BMX* bike. The kid's casual gaze missed Virge's attending to the painted lady, and he nonchalantly peddled up the sidewalk—to confront *me!*

I threw the pole of leaves against the ground like it was a dirty, disgusting thing.

"Whoa!" said the furry adolescent as he stopped next to me. "Is that a huge fucking weed, or what?!"

"Nah," I said, trying desperately to look unconcerned. "We're dumping off some branches. We've been clipping some eucalyptus trees."

The kid averted the gaze of his blood-shot BB eyes only for a second, then flipped a long black lock of greasy hair over the back of his yellow Yamaha shirt.

"Shit!" I thought. "He doesn't believe me… he's not going to leave until I rip off a bunch of leaves and stuff them up his nose as proof it's not dope we're trying to stash!"

The stoner stared at the branch lying at my feet. Sweat beaded on my forehead and palms. He just sat there. "Gotta make small talk," I thought.

"This is the graveyard where the Pink Lady's supposed to be," I said with a crude surfer accent.

"It sure-in-the-fuck is!" The doper exclaimed with a friendly, knowing grin.

"Uh huh," I said toothily.

He just stared.

"Well, later!" I added, with a quick turn back to my "dumping" task.

"Later on!" the kid burped, much to my surprise.

He then rode off down the hill.

I thought for sure he'd be a fly in the ointment. I hoped nothing more would be seen of him and that he wouldn't bring back smelly friends to see the "huge fucking weed."

As my heart slowed, Virge ran up the hill with The Missus fluttering on the protective cardboard backing. Forgetting we were in view, I stopped Virge.

"That loady thought we were bringing in a huge marijuana plant!"

Virge smiled nervously and cocked the five feet of cardboard in front of him to hide it from the street.

"Really? What did you tell him?"

"I told him we were bringing in garbage… tree clippings."

Virge then smiled more broadly.

I raised the pole once more, and we all hurried to the tree of our concern, laden with string, clippers, thread, and a saw, not to mention the flopping "hologram." At the tree, Freddy and Virge hoisted themselves into the branches and began to saw away unwanted limbs. Mindful of activity across the adjacent street, I placed the cardboard backing and screen on the bank out of sight with the pole. "Plop!" went the branches Freddy cut… on the ground, on me. I swept the cuttings into my arms and carefully hid them away under shrubs on the bank. "Plop! Whumpf!" They kept coming down, endlessly.

"Have you gotten enough cut from your way?" I whispered to my easily discernible compatriots framed in the tree.

"Yeah, that's all we should take down," I heard Freddy say.

He waggled his saw.

"Catch!"

The flexible tool hit the ground at my feet with a "plank!"

"Get the pole!"

Following Freddy's instructions, I retrieved our fake branch and thrust it up the sparse eucalyptus. It was swiftly raised out of reach, followed by rustling and grunts.

"It won't come through," Freddy fumed. "Push, Virge!"

"I am!" Virge informed him.

"You guys are going to have to twist it this way…" I scolded. "No! No! Around that other branch!"

"Rustle! Snap! Creak!"

"Shut up! You're making too much noise!" I said.

Just then, subdued talking that came from a condo directly across the street broke into a shouting match.

"What the hell is that?!" I asked myself.

Virge and Freddy momentarily regarded the direction of the yelling and then continued pushing on the pole.

"Shhh!" I hissed.

Craning my head to a gap between the shrubs, I could see through the glowing windows of the condo in question.

"It's nothing!" Freddy insisted.

A girl burst from the condo's front door, slinking across its lawn, belly out, back hunched, face pointed toward the street.

"Someone's coming! Be quiet!" I argued.

"Here Blackie!" the girl whined. "Here Blackie!"

"Good grief! The bitch is looking for her dog!" I thought.

I traced her unsuccessful search until she re-entered the residence a few minutes later.

"Gimme the string!" Freddy called.

"The string!" Virge echoed.

The spool of twine rolled down the bank after I inadvertently kicked it.

"Fuuuuck!" I thought out loud.

Why couldn't I be in that friggin' tree?! Servant boy, that's what I am! "Fuck!" I slipped on the wet succulents and soaked my pants with sprinkler dew. "Shit!" After a short but flagrant hunt, the spool was found and tossed to my comrades. Soon, the branch was lashed in place securely.

"Clump! Clomp!"

The two arboreal pranksters jumped down.

"It looks good!" I told them.

Virge tromped over for a better view, and with a gaping grin replied, "Yeah… Yeah, it does! It looks great!"

He then pranced around a bit, clenched his fists and lips while bending at the knees, and gave his usual, exuberant "Awwright!" followed by several giggles. Freddy just blinked.

The branch did look like part of the tree—at least at night. The only problem was that this tree and its added leaves were different species, and our grafted leaves seemed three times the size and abundance of their living cousins. It also had the wonderful horizontal attitude needed for our Missus, but not inherent in any of the other branches. Would the artificial limb be discovered the next day? Its idiosyncrasies might be easy to see in the daylight hours. Neither Virge nor Freddy seemed too concerned.

Next, we set up to test the hologram. We used a nut weight to throw our ghost's monofilament pull-string over the fake branch from the bank side of the tree after several unsuccessful tries from the opposite direction. I then unpinned the screen from the cardboard, which protected it from the wet of the bank excellently, and tossed the backing with the Missus' sister image face down on top of the hedge, out of sight. The monofilament was then attached to a length of black thread tied to either end of the black antenna spreader. The screen undulated in an almost imperceptible wind, and we tried desperately to keep it from touching the wet grass. The water-based tempera had already brushed off in a few places, and I had repainted the bare spots an exasperating number of times. If the fragile image were to get soaked, that would be the ball game. I wished now that I had had the foresight to use oil-based paints.

Another car passed by into the darkness. From where we were, we could hear light traffic sounds—a cricket chorus as well. There was also the soothing buzz of a lamp on the south-east bend of the graveyard. Its unbroken hum comforted me, as did the thought that this and the many other street lamps presented none of the unwanted light necessary to reveal the screen. But, something else edged into my mind, this time less consoling. In my mind's eye, I could see a big man approaching us from the direction of the lamp. He had an enormous slavering dog straining at its leash. The vision of the bastard's mouth forming "Hey! What are you doing there?!" slowed my breathing to a standstill. And then Freddy grabbed my attention.

"Where's that nut…? Here it is!" he said, plucking the hexagon from the grass. "Give me the thread."

I looked about me, and Virge barked with a shrill note.

"You're standing on it!"

"Damn it!" I cursed.

The black thread drew a zig-zag between blades of grass for yards. How did this happen?! With a few deft movements of my feet, the line became thoroughly tangled around my ankles.

"Fuckin' A!" I snorted.

"Here," Virge grumbled loudly, quiet now thrown to the winds.

The mess was soon alleviated, and we tied the necessary lengths of black line to the nut weights. Freddy drew up the fishing line, which slid easily over the painted limb. The lightweight screen did a half twist in the fall air.

"These nuts aren't heavy enough," said Freddy, more patiently than Virge. "Get some big rocks."

Virge attended pissing, or the pull line, or some other equally remarkable and strenuous feat, while I looked up and down the hedge for stones. I found what amounted to pebbles.

"No!" Freddy cried. "Bigger ones! Those are too small!"

I returned later with a similar cache.

"Couldn't you find any bigger ones?" Freddy asked, now irritated.

"No! There aren't any!" I retorted. "At least I can't find any in the dark!"

"Tomorrow you're gonna have to find some bigger ones when there's better light," he explained.

He then positioned my finds on the anchor lines.

"Pull up a little, Virge."

The screen inched upward and stopped with only a vague wind distortion, which was just fine.

"Now let's shine the light on it," Virge advised. "Freddy, get over there… No, more to the right."

Freddy turned on his plastic lantern. Our ghost looked nothing short of its usual eeriness.

"Virge," I said, "let's go into the graveyard and see where we have the best vantage point to scare Pete. Freddy, when we get over to where we can see, we'll whistle. We'll whistle once to shine the light, twice to turn it off, in case someone comes."

Freddy agreed.

"No!" Virge contested. "Once to turn it off, twice to turn it on."

Freddy wrinkled his brow.

"Okay. Got it, Freddy?" I asked.

"All right," he said.

Hidden by trees on the west border of the graveyard, Virge and I followed the sidewalk to the front gates where we entered and approached Bernardo Yorba's stone. Virge whistled twice, and the image fluttered brightly under the finger-dimmed light of Freddy's lantern.

"Wow! It looks real!" I grinned. "Pete will piss his pants!"

"Yeah!" said Virge, laughing.

"The way it fades in, though… that looks too fake," I said.

I looked around for joggers and the like, and trilled to Freddy.

"Freddy! Flutter your fingers more!"

"What?" came a composed voice from the hedge.

I repeated myself louder, with Virge in unison.

"Flutter your fingers more! It looks too fake when you fade it in and out."

Virge then whistled twice, then once, then twice, forgetting the code. I whistled once. The confusion caused the image to snap off and on, then off again, and then it reappeared with a more misty, materializing effect.

"Great!" I shouted in my most quiet shout.

The hologram was working well. The branches Freddy had cut down gave an opening to a big square of uninterrupted sky through which our illuminating light passed. I expressed my hope to Virge that Freddy would be able to perform as well the next night when Mr. Scalzo came to visit.

As we left, I gazed at the old tombstones and spooky pepper trees standing in the dim moonlight. I wondered if there really *was* a ghost and found my eyes darting to the dark corners near the headstones and beneath the trees. I'm sure that Virge sometimes thought the same thing, although we joked about encountering a real ghost until it was old.

We rejoined Freddy who was standing at the rig.

"It looked great!" I told him. "It should work like a charm."

I then leaped beneath the tree, making motions as if to draw the line down.

"All you need to do after you make it disappear is stay down, pull down the line, roll up the screen, and run off down the bank to Virge's car with the whole thing! If Pete wants to run at the ghost for some reason, or if we want to bring him over here to 'prove' it wasn't a hoax, there won't be a trace of you. You'll be gone before we could get out the front gates running!"

I was beginning to feel elated—this hoax was meant to be. We set up the location perfectly! The screen was taken down, and the limb rescrutinized. It still looked fine.

"Hey, where's this nut?" I asked, pointing to a dangling anchor thread on the screen.

"I dunno," Freddy said.

I dismissed the missing nut and began to walk off to the car, almost forgetting the cardboard. It was retrieved on my remembering stashing it and I pinned the screen back on it. Off to the car we trudged shortly after 10:30 p.m., successful in our deeds.

"I hope Arnie and Midge aren't pissed when we get back late!" I wondered out loud.

"Naaah," Freddy assured me.

Virge thought about what his folks would say, but he had a better alibi with his job.

We gently placed The Missus in the back of the station wagon.

"It's a good thing we're taking two cars to and from the graveyard," I said from the back seat as Freddy and Virge got in. "Pete'll never know Freddy was here."

"What did you tell him?" Freddy inquired.

"I said you had been caught sneaking out to a party recently and that you didn't want to risk sneaking out again."

Freddy laughed. A lot of laughing and joking took place on that ride home. But the mirth ended abruptly when we returned to the Filipos' at 11:00 and found Midge in the kitchen retrieving something from the fridge.

"Did you boys have a good time?" she asked.

I looked at Freddy, thinking he might have perceived something accusative in his mother's voice.

"Yeah!" Freddy said with a smile.

Midge's expression didn't change as it did the last time she suspected we were up to something.

"Good!" she said

Freddy and I clawed through the open refrigerator—I with great relief.

THE DAY OF THE SCARE

Sunday morning, Freddy and his parents went off to "massive Mass-age" at their Catholic church as usual, and I awoke late and bleary-eyed from another late night of TV viewing. I worried very little that day about Pete finding the ghost a prank—or getting everyone arrested—and such indifference on my part was odd. Up until that point, I contemplated both things heavily and discussed them with Freddy and Virge regularly. I felt numbed by the massive undertakings of this joke, and telling Pete it was a stunt after its success was not as appealing as days or maybe weeks of his excitedly reliving his ghost encounter. Halloween was still a few weeks off, but I was distracting myself with thoughts of pumpkin snatching and such. Perhaps this hinted at my doubting the hoax could be pulled off.

That afternoon, Virge and I returned to the cemetery one last time before the scare. First, to satisfy our curiosity about our big branches' daylight appearance, and second, to put aside rocks to weigh down the screen's anchor lines that night.

"Hmmm," I said on seeing the limb. "It still looks remarkably like part of the tree—except the leaves are too long and abundant. And, if you look closely, the brown paint on the pole certainly doesn't match the grayish bark of the tree. And look! Damn! The tree's all lopsided from the cutting you did!"

Virge sat down next to me on a bench we had found not too far from the tree. He started addressing the subject after a glance at the tree. Virge didn't look directly at it, as I was doing. He didn't want to draw any unnecessary attention to it. He spoke in a subdued tone, staring off at the street.

"It looks fine. Nobody will notice."

A jogger passed us. I took in the smell of hot wet grass clippings as they rushed by.

"Don't look at the tree!" Virge warned me in a harsh whisper.

The man jogged by oblivious to the drooping off-color leaves that arched downward from the metal tube seven or eight feet above him.

"Okay," I said. "I believe it. C'mon, let's get some rocks."

We searched more of the hedge, and with poor results.

"Look over along that bank," Virge told me, pointing to a separate hedge near the racquetball courts.

I wandered over to the area he had specified and caught an eyeful of a girl's bottom poking from an open car door. A lovely Japanese girl and her mother emerged from the car as I walked by. The parent was looking around, surveying trees and what have you. She seemed to notice nothing different in our tree either. They walked by me, racquetball rackets in hand.

I found a couple of amply large stones and returned to the cemetery's hedge with the "kerpuck! kerpuck!" of racquetballs behind me. Virge was still half-heartedly looking for rocks when I came up behind him. I placed the ones I had found under the hedge next to the sidewalk.

"Virge!" I called. "I got some good rocks, and I'm putting them here for you and Freddy tonight. Remember where they are."

"Great!" he replied, eyeing the spot where I laid the stones. "Let's go."

"Did you see that girl?" I asked him, using a question as overly used as we were overly sexed.

"What girl?" he asked in a sudden flush of excitement.

"I saw this gorgeous ass poking out of this car door, and this really nice-looking Japanese girl—around sixteen or seventeen—turned around as I walked past."

"Where is she?" Virge inquired frantically.

"Playing racquetball with her mother," I said, pointing to the crest of the concrete courts poking up beyond a grassy knoll.

Virge checked out the girl on our way out and was fortunately less impressed than I was and didn't give his usual stare. He often didn't know the objects of his lust saw him gawking, and it was sometimes embarrassing for those of us with him.

All had gone well on our inspection that morning. I had pretended to go to church so that Virge and I could go to the cemetery again, and my day went like many boring others. That is, until late in the afternoon, when the thought of the quick-approaching scare began gnawing on my nerves. It was getting close to zero hour.

SCARING PETE

After Midge's nutritional dinner of lentil soup, plain lettuce, and incinerated burgers with an extra topping of viscous, brown grease from the frying pan, Freddy and I took our turns in the lavatory with contempt for the violation of our palates and insides.

"Porthole patties again," moaned Freddy. "I almost chunked right there on my plate."

He was as thrilled by Midge's culinary delights as I was.

"Let's get ready for the scare," I replied, releasing a much-needed belch with a few well-placed pats.

Now that Freddy's sister, Ginni, had moved into a studio apartment, we used her empty bedroom's window for quick weekend sneak-outs. Although the window had only a narrow bathroom separating it from Arnie and Midge's bedroom, it proved to be an attractive alternative to sneaking past the parents' open door. The door to the garage at the other end of the house was the farthest from Arnie and Midge, but it clicked and squeaked loudly, no matter how careful we were.

It was dark now. Freddy removed the window screen from Ginni's old room as I watched from the inside. The window was then lifted just a crack to allow easy opening later. The stereo in our adjacent room whined out another one of Doctor Demento's* Demented Discs. I hoped Freddy's parents were as oblivious to our activities as they usually were. So long as the stereo was on, they assumed we were in our room listening to it.

A little after 9:30, Freddy and I retired. At 10:15, Arnie and Midge were still watching TV at the far end of the house. We were lying in our beds almost entirely clothed. Freddy was restless—as I was—with the knowledge that Virge would soon be meeting him at the bottom of the hill after he got off work. With a muffled click, Freddy's clock flipped another little plastic number card: 10:30. Time for Freddy to leave.

Midge's piercing laughter came to me in stereo from down the hall, and from the open window above my bed.

"Haw, Haaw, Haaaaw! Hyuck-yuck!"

The house was a rambling, flat "U" shape, and the windows on each arm were just across the pool from one another. The vibration caused by the pool area made Midge's peculiar guffawing eat into me more than usual.

"Freddy!" I whispered. "They're still up!"

"I know!" he said.

He then lifted his covers, stood up, and began to pull on his jeans.

"Are you gonna go?" I asked.

"I've got to," he said softly, stuffing a pillow under his sheets.

The next thing I knew, Freddy's shadowy form slipped out of our door and into Ginni's bedroom, a denim jacket bundled under one arm. Up went the window with tense, little pushes.

"Screeek! Scrf! Scrf! Scrrrf!"

Then there was a sound of fabric on wood—almost imperceptible. He slid through the window and was gone.

As I waited for my turn, rolling over under my warm covers, I realized it wouldn't be so warm in the cemetery. I'd take the tobacco pipe I had recently started to smoke. The warm bowl felt good in my hand. However, until I left the house unnoticed, such comforts could not be enjoyed. The clock on my nightstand ticked away as though it were the last few moments of my life. "Almost eleven o'clock," I thought. "Almost time to meet Pete."

The night looked darker and more "Octoberish" than when we had erected the artificial limb. I took a deep sniff of the damp earth and green things that filled the air outside my open window… Open window? Arnie always checked our bedroom for an open window to keep us from "catching cold." Damned if he wouldn't come in here and close it, like always, noticing at the same time that we were gone! I took one last look at the big pines along the back fence, a farewell sniff of the garden and a quick look at my spindly pumpkin plants outside, and pulled the window tightly shut. The clock radio with the flip-cards that normally faced Freddy's bed now stared me in the face with its bright colon eyes. 10:45, 10:46, 10:47. Suddenly, there was a movement at our door, dimly lit by a light down the hall. ARNIE!

Arnie's prickly gourd poked into our bedroom, and I pretended to be asleep. He hadn't been coming to check on the window lately because we had been keeping it shut—that's why Freddy took the chance of leaving while his parents were still up. But, we didn't take into account that Arnie might have felt the draft! I expected our bright bedroom light to come on, but somehow nothing happened.

"SHIT!" I thought. "Either he suspects something or…"

His silhouette vanished as fast as it had appeared.

"…He felt a draft!"

Seeing the window closed, Freddy's father left none the wiser. Moments later, he and Midge finished bedding down. All the lights went out, and everything was silent.

11:01, 11:02, 11:03! Time to go! Every dormant muscle came alive as I rose from my bed. The bed springs audibly groaned. I got up more slowly.

The pillow-dummy "Freddy" in the other bed that the real one had so hastily made looked rumpled and flat. I made my dummy more carefully— heftier—and then slipped on my old blue denim jacket. As quietly as I could, I then snuck into the next bedroom where my exit lay. I tripped on something near the window but didn't come close to going down. It made no noise, so I immediately eased out of the window.

From the top of the driveway, I could see no sign of Pete on Rose Drive, but on approaching the bottom, I found him hunched in the driver's seat of his faded yellow VW Beetle. He had parked inconspicuously near the south-east corner of the Filipos' property, near a ditch where the shadows of trees hid him.

"Hi, Pete!" I chirped, opening the car door and startling the hell out of him.

"Agh! Oh! Oh, God! You scared me!" he gasped, gripping his scrawny, heaving chest.

"Sorry," I said.

"Don't do that again!"

"Okay," I said apologetically. "You must be pretty anxious about going out to the graveyard!"

"Yeah, I am," he admitted.

"Did you have any trouble finding this place?"

"No. Not really."

"I hope you don't mind if I smoke on our way over there," I said, pulling out my brier-wood pipe.

"No. No, I don't…"

I think he lied.

"…You don't have any 'funny stuff' in there, do you?" he asked.

"No," I replied, "but I kind of wish I did—that graveyard's a scary place. It might be cooler if I were really mellow."

Pete looked away, a bit peeved and nervous. He seemed a bit paranoid about everything. It was still early, and I needed to do some stalling to allow Virge and Freddy to get into position.

"Are you ready to go?" Pete asked.

"Well, I think I owe you an explanation about why you have to park down here."

"I know," he said callously. "Freddy's parents won't allow you to do what you want."

I didn't actually dislike Arnie and Midge, so I took about five minutes to explain their standpoint as guardians and ours as delinquents. Pete listened quietly, seeming to understand. I then inquired what time it was.

"Uh, about eleven o'clock," he answered.

Freddy and Virge probably needed more time to set up, so I started a more reciprocating conversation on the guards that supposedly made their rounds near the cemetery. These mistruths lasted only a few minutes, but Pete became quite bug-eyed.

"And, that's why none of us will be carrying any flashlights," I finished.

Pete nodded.

By now, Virge and Freddy were putting up the screen. I still needed to give them an edge…

"Y'know, Pete, if we're going to be sitting out in that damp graveyard for a while, we'll need something to sit on."

"Yeah," he agreed.

"I should get some towels from the house."

"All right," he said after a short hesitation.

I think he would have liked to have left by now.

Exiting Pete's car, I remembered that I had put towels for this specific purpose on the floor in Ginni's bedroom. I then walked up the steep driveway through the grove and into the dark shadows of the slat dividers and patio roof outside the room. I lightened my step past Arnie and Midge's window on the way there.

After reopening Ginni's window, I stuck my head in and felt around for the towels I had placed near the baseboard. They weren't there! Damn it! That's what I tripped over—I had kicked them out of the way! I dismissed the idea of re-entering the house to search the room and wasted some more time by walking out to a clothesline by the utility sheds. I retrieved two damp pool towels there. At Virge's, across the way, I could have sworn there was a light on. Were his parents up? No. It was the bathroom light the Farises left on for their boys all these years. It was shining through a crack in Jake's bedroom drapes. Poor Jake. He was asleep, missing out on all the fun.

Back at Pete's car, I tossed the towels on the back seat and received his glad nod.

"I don't think we'll see anything tonight," I comforted him. "But it sure was terrifying to see that thing… and on a night when it's not supposed to be around, too!"

I just repeated what I had told Pete at work in the past week. Supposedly, Virge and I had seen an eerie specter at the graveyard in a month it was not reported to appear.

"I still think you guys have some kind of ESP that allows you to see things other people can't," Pete insisted.

I had heard this more than once before. By now, it was pissing me off for some reason.

"Not me!" I said. "Maybe Virge. He's a strange one! Always acting spacey, almost removed from the environment around him sometimes."

Pete rubbed franticly at the condensation inside his windshield with his bare knuckles.

"Here," I said, tossing him a towel.

"Thanks."

"Shall we go to the graveyard now?"

"Yes," Pete said, relieved that we were now ready. "Which way is it?"

I lit my bowl of cherry blend and pointed south.

"That way. Yorba Linda Boulevard."

And so we were off, a little late even. Pete's gold-rimmed spectacles couldn't hide his apprehension. No doubt, he was worried about meeting ghoulies and ghosties, and especially long-leggity guardsies—and all in an old graveyard, too! The picture I had painted about the place had sparked Pete's nervous interest in it and its legendary ghost or he wouldn't have been there that night. Well, Mr. Scalzo wouldn't be disappointed!

My navigation went well, and Pete and I arrived in the neighborhood around the cemetery right on time: 11:30 p.m.

"Where's the graveyard?" Pete asked.

He found it hard to comprehend that an old Spanish cemetery managed to hide in this neighborhood full of homes.

"Virge had told me this place had changed, but this is incredible!" I said, denying any recent visits.

I pointed to the graveyard's west bank of trees and big shrubs.

"There it is!"

"That's it?" Pete asked incredulously.

"Yeah," I said. "Park here. This looks like a good spot."

We got out of Pete's car on just the spot where we had unloaded the big branch.

"Where's Virge?" I asked myself aloud. "He said he'd meet us here by the tennis courts."

I scratched my short beard in some concern. The street was deathly still. There were no joggers, no furry BMX jockeys, or any other people for that matter. Nor were there the usual abundance of brightly lit windows among the condos. No traffic sounds, no crickets, just the same "tack! tack! tack!" of a few moths and beetles bouncing off the light near the tennis courts. Everything looked ideal for the scare, and luckily, no thanks to Steve Sabine (the drunken rat!), I was in a good mood for some acting.

"There's Virge!" I blurted.

No doubt Pete had already seen the "sullen" figure scuff down the bank. Virge was already trying to behave "differently." He approached us, looking off and very far away.

"Pete," I said, "Virge Faris. Virge, Pete Scalzo."

The two shook hands and exchanged greetings, and we started up the grassy slope to the sidewalk that led to the front gates of the cemetery. On the way, Virge was to begin the "psychic chitchat" that I had told him would be useful. I started the discussion by trying to make Virge look like a frequent graveyard visitor, and stuck by what I had told Pete at work.

"Virge's been to the cemetery several times with buddies from school recently," I told Pete. "Haven't you, Virge?"

"No," said Virge flatly.

I looked at Virge emphatically, knowing one of us had to renege. I made the wide-eyed, remember-what-we-talked-about stare.

"But I thought you said…"

"No. Nuh uh!" Virge insisted.

Fuck me! What was Virge doing? Oh, what a damned tangled web I had woven! I had totally forgotten that we agreed Virge was to be presented as twenty-two and not seventeen to give him a little more credibility.

"You came here last year after Troy games with a bunch of other kids a lot, didn't you?!"

"Yeah," he said. "But that was a long time ago."

Seeing my disgust, poor Virge quickly confronted the eye-batting and slightly bewildered Pete.

"I had an experience a while back," Virge said. "It was really strange. I've had a lot of things like that happen."

"Shit!" I thought. "That was heavily veiled!" I quickly interrupted this would-be conversation and moved the subject to the ghostly matters at hand.

"Yeah, well, uh… we saw something two years ago… that night we got drunk, remember?"

"Oh yeah!" Virge said, acknowledging another famous lie.

"Remember how fast we ran?" I chuckled. "I tripped over you and fell flat on my ass!"

Virge laughed convincingly.

"Yeah," Virge replied. "You were so excited you couldn't even get the car door open!"

I was beginning to think I'd have to be a real buffoon tonight to live up to the cowardly image that was being created. That's all right. Through all of this, Pete seemed only vaguely amused.

"From what Slade tells me, Virge, you might have some ESP abilities."

Virge gave his bashful wince, breaking character, and I prayed he wouldn't give vent to his usual "golly!" or "gee-whiz!" I suppose the few months that he had been exposed to the combination of both Freddy and me cured him of such unsophisticated responses. His answer was proof.

"Hell, I don't know," Virge responded.

Pete smiled.

"No, really!"

This exchange was getting smarmy, so I intervened with a question directed at the blushing Mr. Faris.

"Where's your car?"

Virge turned south and pointed.

"Over on the other side," he said. "I didn't want any of the guards to know there was somebody here."

"Do you think maybe we should move my car?" Pete asked me.

"Nah!" I replied. "It's fine where it is."

"Maybe we should get inside!" Pete suggested to our astonishment.

"Okay," I said, "but get a load of this gate! Gnarled vines, looming tree, real classic stuff, huh?"

"Yeah," Pete answered with a sheepish grin.

Pointing to the marker out front, I repeated its name and date for him.

"Yorba Historical Cemetery, established 1858… Home of the infamous Pink Lady."

"Home of the Whopper!" Virge interjected, using a Burger King slogan.

"Yeah! A helluva ghost!" I said with a smile. "Look at these gates…"
I pushed on one of the heavy iron doors, and it made a delicious creak.
Pete looked pale.

We entered through the metal tunnel-shaped trellis.

"Damn!" I burst out. "Fuckin' people have been coming in here to
drink beer!"

I kicked an old six-pack carton resting on a pile of glass shards.

"I wish they'd lock those gates," I said.

Pete was convinced of the cemetery's regular visitation and was looking all
around him, as Virge was. I pointed to the condominium complex east of us.

"That's where the guards are," I warned.

Virge's eyes met mine with unabashed humor. Pete turned to look where I
was pointing. I could have sworn I saw him swallow hard.

"They have a station in those condos for the safety of the tenants and
to look out for the graveyard," I said. "I think they only come around on
nights that are really bad for vandalism. You know. Fridays and Saturdays—
game nights. They've got guns and flashlights and have a regular route
around the graveyard."

I panned my arm around the four corners of the small cemetery.

"I think they usually come around at midnight. If you see a flashlight,
it's probably a guard, but I don't think they'll be a problem on a quiet
night like this."

Now Pete looked flush, sick.

"Let's show Pete around," Virge suggested softly.

"Okay," I said with the hint of a smile.

During the time we walked around the cemetery, I pointed out the
damaged tombstones to Pete. One vandal had broken the head off a lamb,
exquisitely carved in marble by an artisan six decades earlier. He seemed as
bothered by the damage as I was. Then, Virge ushered us to the area where
we believed the Pink Lady had her grave. We pored over a few of the many
headstones under an old pepper there.

"This area feels cold," I remarked. "It makes me shudder."

Pete was more than willing to follow Virge out of this area when
Virge suggested a walk down the inside of the west hedge. The cemetery
was as dark and damp as usual. Pete was naturally soaking in its "horror
movie" qualities.

"I feel kind of nervous," I said.

"So do I," Virge echoed.

"Me too," Pete confessed.

It was sufficiently dark that we had to be careful navigating through the tombstones and around the crypts. It was difficult to see anything.

"Look at all this tomb grass!" I said.

"And these branches…" Virge added.

We passed under more pepper trees with low, weeping branches.

"Yeah!" I said. "They keep brushing against my neck. It's giving me the creeps!"

"Yeah!" mimed Pete, brushing a fern-like limb from his face. "They're brushing my head, too!"

Then a low branch—bang!

"Oooh!" I groaned. "I just hit my head!"

Maybe Pete was the more fortunate being of smaller stature than Virge and me. We were both over six feet tall.

"End of the trail!" Virge informed us.

I grinned like a fiendish jack-a-lantern.

"Ah! Back past the Pink Lady's grave!"

We turned around and retraced our steps on the trail, which was really just an indentation between clumps of mondo grass. I was especially watchful of my head.

At the middle of the graveyard, Virge and I showed Pete the massive tombstone of Bernardo Yorba and those of his relatives surrounding it.

"This man," Virge stated, "owned most of the area that's now Placentia and Yorba Linda."

"Before California was even a state," I added.

Pete seemed impressed.

"It gives me the creeps being around all these graves full of dead people," I said, hopping away on one foot, wary of the sunken mounds on either side.

"Slade, these are only the shells of people!" Virge corrected me. "They aren't really here."

I guess Virge wanted Pete to think he had special insight on the afterlife or something.

"Pete," I ventured, pointing to the eastern park lawn, "that's where Virge and I saw the ghost back in '78."

"Yeah?" he asked, intrigued.

"Well, like I said before, it was just a field then. No houses. But it was out there, looking straight at us! And, it didn't have any legs! It was kind of partially materialized!"

Virge nodded in affirmation and retold the cute story about how fast we ran, tripping, and falling. Pete seemed more amused this time.

"Let's find a place to sit down and wait," I said. "I brought some towels to sit on."

And sit on them we did, right on Bernardo Yorba's grave, along with a few weathered plastic gardenias in a coffee can.

"I don't think we'll see anything tonight," I said, pretending to reassure myself.

Pete seemed to agree.

We were sitting on the grave's concrete surface on the south side of the big tombstone, and I was secretly reveling in the thought that Freddy was out there, somewhere—behind the hedge, behind a tree or shrub, lurking all around.

"This cement is uncomfortable," I said. "Let's move over near those juniper trees."

Virge and Pete agreed. The curb-like crypt's edge by the trees felt better on our backsides. Unfortunately, we couldn't see the tree where we rigged our ghost.

"What time is it?" I asked Pete.

"Uh… twelve-thirty," he said.

"It's damp over here!" I complained again. "Let's go toward the middle more."

Again we moved, this time finally. On our way over, I asked Virge in the faintest whisper what time Freddy would put on the show.

"I told him a little over an hour after you guys got here, like you said," Virge whispered back.

That sounded good. If the ghost were to appear in our first few minutes there, it would seem suspicious.

After each of us had crept off to piss in the hedge, we squatted near a couple of concrete grave markers that were flush with the ground and made casual remarks about their oldness. Virge was on Pete's left, and I was on his right. All of us faced south where the ghost rig was set up.

I could see the screen! It was hung smack in the middle of the patch of sky created by the defoliated tree, maybe twenty-five yards away. I could see the thin black metal support and an area of the sky just a shade darker than the rest, that was it. It wasn't noticeable if you weren't looking for it specifically. I looked at Virge. He was looking elsewhere. I didn't think Virge had seen it, and I know Pete hadn't. I was getting cold and felt edgy.

Then there was a sound.

"Spfft! Spfft! Spfft!"

"I wonder what that noise is!" I said.

"What noise?" Pete asked.

"That hissing noise. Hear it?"

"Spfft! Spfft! Spfft!"

It came again very quietly.

"Sprinklers," Virge suggested.

He was right.

"That's a relief!" I said, feigning fear.

Just then, we all jumped at another sound that gave us all a start.

"MEOW!"

"A cat!" I declared.

"Oh!" said Pete, expending a pent-up breath. "Only a cat."

It was from Freddy. Freddy was good at making a specific cat sound, though formed the same way someone would do the voice of Donald Duck. I worried he might give us away with the crawling around he was doing. He must have been bored with waiting.

"What time is it, Pete?"

"Twelve thirty-six."

"We're going to have to leave soon," I reminded him.

"Yeah," he sighed.

"Let's stay a little longer, though—until about quarter of. That okay with you, Virge?"

"Okay," Virge smirked.

"All right!" I said.

Shortly before 12:45, I glanced at Virge again, who to my surprise was giving me "the look." His face showed he was bursting with anticipation, and his eyes jerked south once, signaling me to look there. There was The Missus bright and clear! It looked like she was standing directly over the hedge, instead of below the tree!

"What's that?!" I erupted, jumping to my feet.

"What?" Pete asked excitedly.

"Over there!" I cried.

Both of my colleagues were now standing.

"OH, MY GOD!" I screeched, pointing, "There it is! We've got to get out of here!"

Virge reeled away from us, squelching a bomb-burst of laughter.

Pete just froze.

"My God! There *IS* something!" he said in astonishment.

I stamped and screamed to draw Pete's attention away from any flaws in the rig.

"MY GOD! MY GOD!" I howled. "IT'S THE GHOST! LET'S GO!"

Pete wouldn't (or couldn't) turn away. An icy wave of terror had crested on his scalp, and what little hair he had on top of his head was standing on end. He turned to me with an extremely earnest look.

"Shhh! Shhh! Be quiet!" he and Virge implored, not wanting to attract any attention.

We stood staring at it a moment, and then the image changed at the top and bottom simultaneously, thanks to the movement of Freddy's fingers on the flashlight lens. It looked like a reflection on water, eaten up by ripples until it disappeared completely. There was not one illuminated leaf during the whole forty-five-second presentation. It was exquisite!

We all stood in silence for a minute or two. Pete was dumbfounded.

"I actually saw a ghost," he said finally and somewhat somberly.

"Let's go!" I whined. "Let's go!"

Freddy must have been enjoying my noise greatly.

"All right! All right!" Virge said.

Once we were out of the cemetery, Pete was wringing his hands and staring off into space.

"I can't believe I actually saw a ghost!"

I, for one, thought it would be a great idea to take Pete over to where Freddy had been. I wanted an impromptu search for "hoaxers" and voiced it plainly.

"Virge!" I moaned. "I've got to go over there to prove to myself that it wasn't a hoax!"

Pete, whom I had left behind with a short jog in the rig's direction, looked at me as if to say 'that bastard's got balls!'

"If that was a hoax, it was a damned good one!" was Pete's response.

Virge quickly acted as if to settle me by running over to me. He grabbed my arm, and with his back to Pete said, "Slade, calm down!" Then murmured, "Tell Freddy to set it back up!"

"No!" I yelled to satisfy Pete's ogling. "I want you guys to come, too! I want to prove to myself it wasn't a hoax! Somebody would have to leave traces!"

Of course, Freddy hadn't left traces—at least I was pretty sure he hadn't—and I wanted Pete to see for himself that there was not a trace of human trickery. A pièce de résistance you could call it. Virge glared at me, gripping my arm harder.

"See if Freddy can set it up again!" he whispered.

"No!" I yelled, "Come with me!"

Virge wasn't thrilled. He wanted to double the fun with another sighting—or to let Pete off the hook.

"Virge," I said in a hushed tone, "there's no way we can set it back up! The line's all down, and it'll take too long. Besides, it may not fool him again."

"C'mon," Virge hissed.

"All right. Okay," I said. "Wait here."

I trotted down the west sidewalk and peered around the corner to where Freddy had been. Not a trace. He had gone down the bank with the whole setup less than fifteen seconds after he shut off his flashlight, as planned. It would've been ridiculous to try to re-rig the ghost.

I quietly called Freddy's name a few times and walked back to the plot of grass where Virge and Pete waited. But, on the way, a fleeting figure caught my eye. "Shit!" I thought. "He must think we want Pete to have a sporting chance at blowing our cover!" Freddy was scampering around the street below, hunching over as he ran with the bundle of screen under his arm. If Pete had been with me, he surely would have seen him.

"Nothing," I said dolefully on my return.

Pete thought my proclamation ambiguous at best but didn't question it. Virge knew what I meant, and gave up hope of re-enacting the scare.

"Uh, maybe we should leave, guys," Pete suggested.

"Yes. Maybe we could get some coffee, though," I offered.

Virge forlornly agreed.

I ran off to Pete's car, forgetting Freddy would have to wait around the graveyard until Virge came back to pick him up.

"Just follow Virge down this street to the 7-11," I told Pete, heaving a towel onto the back seat. "Man, am I tired."

"So am I," conceded Pete, who then quickly regained his train of thought. "I still can't believe it!"

"Didn't I tell you we were telling the truth?" I implored.

"Yes, there's no doubt about it. I actually saw a real ghost!" Pete said. Trailing Virge out of the vicinity, we soon found ourselves at the nearby mini-mart. It was closed, and it was 1:00 a.m.

"Let's go to Bob's," Virge called from his car window.

"Okay," I answered. "Just follow Virge, Pete. We're going to Bob's Big Boy in Placentia. It'll be open."

I had entirely forgotten about poor Freddy. No doubt his knees were knocking in the cold of the cemetery. With all the jabbering about supernatural crap Pete was doing, I couldn't think straight. All the way down Imperial Highway it was "incorporeal" this, and "astral" that. I began to feel very guilty. I knew he'd tell everyone at work about the ghost at his first chance. I warned him to have good judgment about who he confided in—if he confided in anyone before I could tell him it was a fake! I should have done it right then and there.

"You know, Pete, when Virge and I saw the ghost years ago, we went and told all our friends."

"Yeah?"

"And… Well, they just didn't believe us—even though we were telling the truth. And, uh, we just looked like fools! Everyone laughed at us!"

"I see."

"I wouldn't go telling everyone if I were you. It could be embarrassing!"

"Yeah. Yeah," Pete said. "I won't. I'll just tell the people I really think will believe me—like Rob." (Pete's supervisor at Volt.)

Famous last words. Would our "pigeon" become one of the formidable "stool" variety?!

Once at Bob's, we were all disappointed to find it closed, too. A waitress who was leaving informed us that the restaurant closed at 1:00 a.m. but told us to try a Denny's.

"Naw," Virge said when I recommended we find the far-off place. "Let's try another 7-11, there's one on Placentia Avenue, I think."

Tagging along behind Virge again, we found the next mini-mart open and converged on two parking spaces before its brightly-lit doors. On the way there, I suggested we draw pictures of what we had seen at the graveyard. I rummaged through the papers in Pete's glove compartment as we stopped, looking for something like a drawing pad and pencil. I only succeeded in knocking my teetering pipe from its place there, scattering its embers.

"Damn it!" I groused.

"Here," Pete huffed. "Here's a pencil..."

He withdrew a ratty, tooth-marked specimen from a corner of the glove compartment I had missed.

"And use the back of this—it's no good," Pete instructed. "Don't use *that*! That's my registration papers!"

I took the crumpled paper and pencil he poked at me, and we all trudged into the 7-11 under the mistrusting eyes of the lone cashier who was sweeping up.

In the store, Virge was milling about with a funny look on his face.

"We've seen a ghost!" he piped at the cashier, much to my astonishment.

Pete was quick to supplement the statement with a bright gaze. The man must have thought us quite odd, if not dangerously insane.

"Oh yeah?" he said.

"Yeah!" Virge bleated.

I wanted to make us seem less annoying.

"We've been at the Yorba Linda cemetery tonight, and we saw something... I don't know what. We just came in for some coffee."

The mini-mart fellow wasn't relieved by my comment but strained a polite smile at us. I scanned a row of dirty magazines, suggesting my interest didn't lie in conversation, but in the array of smut.

After filing by a self-serve coffee machine and doling out some legal tender, we went back outside into the hushed October morning. Virge had left the ghost's enormous cardboard backing on the back seat of his car. It was plain to see to all of us as we walked by it, but I was shocked to see the cardboard shudder as I passed. Freddy wasn't back at the graveyard waiting for Virge to return and help him retrieve the big branch. He was in Virge's car under the cardboard!

"Good Lord!" I thought, somewhat amused. I hoped no one had seen me reel from the car door, yet I was tired of seeing how long we could sustain the charade. I almost wanted Pete to find Freddy at this point, and end the whole fiasco.

"Let's find a flat place to write," Pete urged.

"How about the tailgate?" Virge asked, pointing to the back of his station wagon.

"That's good," said Pete.

In no time, Virge had the gate open, and Pete was kneeling at his makeshift desk. Of course, Pete's line of vision included Freddy's cardboard blanket. The board quivered. Pete was looking at it, too! Nothing. Pete scratched his chin.

"Let's see… Lt's October 5th… er, 6th now… 1980, and the ghost appeared at 12:44 a.m."

"Approximately," I reminded him.

"Yeah. Approximately."

The young cashier was now outside, glancing at us every now and again as he hosed the sidewalk. He may have interpreted our loitering as part of an eventual robbery of the store—either that, or loonies fascinated him. He kept watching us.

"Let's draw some sketches of what we saw," I said. "You go first, Virge."

Virge took Pete's pencil stump, and with a tight grip on the chew marks, carefully rendered a rough outline of how he knew our ghost painting looked.

"Hmmm… very interesting," Pete mumbled.

"Your turn," I told him.

Pete flecked the paper for a few moments, then leaned back to accommodate our view. I was disappointed. His drawing looked like a luminous basketball with a softball head and dark, slanted eyes. I sniggered to myself. It certainly wasn't the embodiment of evil we were going for!

Now it was the artist's turn. I sketched a voluptuous Spanish woman even more closely resembling the hologram than Virge's example. Pete's eyebrows fused.

"You know," he said, "I didn't see as much detail as you guys did. You must sense more than I can."

"Well, I know I saw arms, hair—even clothing," I replied. "Some kind of circular sash, too."

"Yeah! Come to think of it, I saw something on the waist, too," Pete said.
I turned to Virge.

"Virge saw about the same thing I did, I guess."

"Uh huh," Virge smiled. "I saw arms and stuff."

"Yours looks like the Pillsbury dough-boy!" I told Pete, scoffing at his drawing. "Didn't you see arms?"

We all looked at Pete's sketch. Two little diagonal marks suggested our Missus' armpits, but Pete refused to believe they were part of any appendages.

"Maybe clothing," he said.

"Naw! Arms!" I insisted.

Virge and I were both enjoying the conversation and drawing session. I know he wanted to laugh as much as I did. We were all exhausted, though. Pete and I drove back to the Filipos' house with Freddy's hiding place still unknown to Pete. We followed Virge's car.

Pete pulled up to the bottom of Freddy's hill near Virge, who was standing on the sidewalk in the dark shadows of the row of pines there.

"Thanks for driving us over there," I told Pete as I moved from his Beetle to the passenger door of Virge's car, which was still open from Freddy's exit. "It was one helluva night! We'll have to go again sometime, or find another graveyard or something."

"Yeah," Pete sighed. "That was really something. I still don't believe it!"

"Well, believe it!" I grunted.

Virge trundled up behind me.

"Nice meeting you, Virge," Pete called out.

"Nice meeting you!" Virge replied. "We ought to do this again sometime!"

They laughed halfheartedly.

Hopefully, we wouldn't be doing another stunt like this soon—especially with Pete as the mark. He had enough to blab about now.

"Good night, Pete," I said blearily. "See you tomorrow at work."

"Good night!" he echoed with the slam of his car door.

Pete again attacked the moisture on the inside of his windshield with his knuckles. He then drove off down Rose Drive, looking like the tired cat that ate the canary.

It was a job well done.

"Was it worth it, Virge?" I inquired.

"I guess," Virge offered with a puff of dragon-like vapor spreading on the night air.

I was tired like Virge, but more stimulated by the night's activities. Perhaps it would have been more fun if we had pulled the proverbial wool over the eyes of a group, or even a city, rather than just an individual. But, for our first attempt at a hoax, Pete was a good start. A good experiment.

"Did you see him wet his pants!" I asked Virge with a laugh.

"No. Did he?"

"Yeah! But just a little bit. He was trying hard to keep it hidden with one of the towels."

We walked up the driveway now, away from Virge's car, not as quiet as might have been appropriate for a sneak-out night.

"Where's Freddy?" I asked.

With that, there was a sudden "Wheeee!" and the whoosh of a ghost in front of us. "Plop!" The cardboard backer smacked the driveway, launched from behind an orange tree by a chuckling Freddy.

"There you are!" I chirped. "You were great! The ghost worked perfectly! Oh, and the way it disappeared!"

I waggled my fingers with my hands facing one another, drawing them slowly together until they meshed.

"Just like that!" I squealed. "Hey, I didn't know you were in Virge's car! I saw the cardboard move! I freaked!"

Freddy looked at me as if to say 'what an idiot!' Freddy's impromptu hidden transportation setup had been arranged with Virge unbeknownst to me. I had assumed Virge would break from Pete and me at one point and go back to the cemetery to pick him up.

Our praise about the scare was brief.

"I'm going back to get the branch!" Virge announced.

"Tonight?" I asked. "What for?"

"Why?" Freddy asked with concern.

"I might as well," Virge answered. "I've got the car and everything."

"Well, Freddy and I have to go to school and work tomorrow," I said. "We've got to go to bed—it's almost 2:00 a.m.!"

Virge's hopes for help in retrieving his precious pool pole were dashed against the tombstones like a rotten pumpkin.

"We'll help you get it tomorrow night," I offered.

"Okay," Virge said. "Tomorrow."

Virge then drove around the corner to home, and Freddy and I climbed back through Ginni's window and got into our respective beds, exhausted. Arnie's snoring was good to hear. It told us there had been no unfortunate discoveries.

THE FALLOUT

The next couple of weeks were sheer hell. The following day, Monday, I walked into work to find that the artists who had come in early had already heard all the details of our "sighting." Pete must have run between cubicles shouting about it for it to have spread so fast.

When I entered my work area, there were random stares in my direction from coworkers I scarcely knew. "He's the one!" they'd whisper to one another. I could tell things were going to be crazy. Pete, in his cube behind me, was busily sketching a dough-man at his desk for a few fascinated females. He must have been in heaven.

It was now 7:00 a.m. Time to work. I wondered if old Bob Arnel, the head supervisor, would stand on a chair and angrily shout "All right, people, time to get to work!" He did this on a similar occasion when something caused widespread idleness and talking. Well, where was the bastard?

People flocked to Pete's desk all day. Some would tease him, taunt him, ridicule him. Luckily, I received a modest amount of attention in comparison to the ridicule Pete had brought upon himself.

One of the display ad artists and Volt clown, Larry McAvery, was the first of the Christians to jump me:

"Pete said you and he went to a graveyard and saw a ghost," he chided me, showing his perfect pearly whites.

"We saw something!" I replied, not offering any details.

I knew that born-again Christians like Larry believe that you either go to Heaven or Hell when you die—hanging around here on Earth isn't possible or isn't allowed. To them, any spirit that's earthbound is one of Satan's personal legion of demons. Go figure!

"C'mon, what are you guys trying to pull?" he admonished me.

"Nothing!" I said.

The fool left on seeing my annoyance, only to pester Mr. Scalzo again a short time later.

Sarah, a lovely girl whom I secretly adored, and Karen, her constant companion, had confirmed the legend of the Pink Lady to Pete before the scare. They were among the few to believe Pete's story, but they only allowed a few hushed earfuls of it at a time. The ruckus its first telling created had everyone particularly careful not to be seen doing any more talking on Volt time.

Another person who believed Pete was a Christian girl, Laura. Laura professed to Pete that she knew the ghost was a demon, and that Pete was in danger of being possessed by seeing it. But Laura was ignored. She was rumored to have had a history of emotional breakdowns, and at one time she had confided in Pete that she was running from her former church's members as one might run from the police or the Mob.

As the week wore on, Pete was finding that even the most interested of his coworkers were becoming bored with the retelling of his story and his conjecture about the spirit world. His little dough-boy drawings and pages of statistics soon found an honored place in the back of his Volt taboret drawer. I felt bad. I really did. I had intended to tell Pete the whole thing was a fake that Monday morning. I didn't dare announce it as a fraud now. How was I to know Pete would blab like this, and before 7:00 a.m., too!

I should have been burnt out from the late night scaring Pete, but I wasn't due to all the commotion at work and the guilt I was experiencing. I helped to pick up Pete's spirits by passing him little notes, asking questions:

"Why do you think the ghost chose to manifest itself to us at that time?" I'd query.

"You or Virge must have some extrasensory power that you don't realize!" Pete would answer.

Steve Sabine saw us passing the notes and observed Pete's gathering depression that Monday. He couldn't help getting his digs in.

"Have you ever heard of the famous 'Midget Ghost of Brea?'" he asked Pete.

Pete's eyes widened.

"Really?"

"Yes!" Steve said. "It's supposed to be seen in a drainage ditch off of Brea Boulevard. It runs out of a sewer pipe shouting, 'think of dental hygiene,' waving a little toothbrush."

Steve waved his hands and wiggled like a cheap floozy.

"People just shit when they see it!" he continued. "He's three feet tall, has a camera, sandals, and a Hawaiian-print shirt with surfers on it."

Pete hardly appreciated Steve's humor. I couldn't help but roar with uncontrollable laughter (In fact, this was so funny that I drew the cartoon shown below.)

Later that day, Pete still looked depressed, and all I could say was "I told you so."

"People won't believe you!" I reminded him. "Didn't I tell you that?"

Pete would nod dolefully.

A few glances to the supervisor's area and more notes were passed, slipped, and sneaked.

Pete left work that day feeling only slightly better in some final knowledge I had left with him.

"You know what you saw, Pete—can there be any doubt what it was?"

That evening, Virge and Pete and I met at the graveyard again. I had told Pete that we would take photos of the precise area where the ghost had appeared over the hedge. Pete met me at the Filipos' shortly after work,

and we soon intercepted Virge and Jake at the cemetery. We took photos of Pete pointing from where we had sat at the time of the sighting to a point above the hedge, where the ghost appeared to have been. The eucalyptus tree beyond was still heavy with the camouflaged pool pole. Even though Pete looked in its direction, he noticed nothing unusual. We also investigated the ground and hedge on that south side of the cemetery, debating the possibility that the trees in the vicinity could help in a hoax. Even under the drooping pole, Pete only saw what he wanted to see. The sight of the pole also reminded Virge and me that we needed to retrieve it.

We took more pictures with Pete's instamatic, some of where Virge and I had supposedly seen the Pink Lady in '78. Others were taken to show the relative size of the ghost from our scare-night vantage point, with Virge and me standing side by side and pointing to a spot a foot above the hedge. All of this was for Pete's satisfaction, though we did get a raggedy-ass kick out of milking the whole thing. We presented a pink oleander flower to Pete in remembrance of our "great sighting." Pete left the graveyard giving every appearance that he felt like a new man.

The next day, Tuesday, Virge and Freddy and I got together at our frequent meeting place in Virge's bedroom.

"Did you hear what happened last night?" Virge asked me in an excited tone.

"No," I retorted. "What happened?"

Virge grinned.

"A cop stopped me last night!"

"Really?" I exclaimed. "Where?"

Freddy looked on, complacently.

"On Imperial Highway!" Virge said. "I saw these flashing lights in my rearview mirror, and I thought, 'Oh, shit! He's going to stop me'—and he did!"

"What did you do, Virge?!" I inquired with alarm.

"He asked me what I had in the back, and I said, 'branches.' He wanted to see, so I got out and showed him the pole. He seemed satisfied and told me to watch how far things stuck out of the back of my car."

"Heh, heh!" Virge chuckled. "I had tied a white handkerchief to the pole, so there wasn't much he could do. He couldn't give me a ticket or anything."

"Wow!" I sniggered. "He either thought you were stealing trees from a nursery or transporting a huge pot plant! It's good there wasn't any snagged stuff in the back!"

After the initial surprise of Virge's story, I went on to explain Pete's behavior at work the previous day, and we all had a hearty laugh.

In the following week, Pete accumulated magazines and books concerning Southern California ghosts, most of which were supplied by sympathetic friends at work who had forgiven his initial mania. He spent a lot of his free time deciding which graveyard to visit next. There was a phantom bulldog in San Juan Capistrano and a ghostly stagecoach that occasionally crossed the Santa Ana Freeway. But to Pete's amazement, I showed very little interest in staking out these places.

About two weeks after the scare, Pete "cleared up" the ghost-sighting rumors for his Volt supervisor, Rob. Rob supposedly possessed a certain amount of ESP and belonged to some sort of secretive society concerning extrasensory powers. I had always considered Rob a strange fish, but I never had any real basis for it. He just seemed a little weird.

Pete urged me to back him up in confirmation of our Pink Lady sighting. (Okay. What the hell.)

We approached Rob, and I said something foolish like "Hi, I'm the guy who saw the spirit with Pete. Pete and I were the sighters and the ghost was the, uh, 'sightee.'" Rob looked at me suspiciously. He had unnerving pale blue eyes that seemed to bore right through me. I was sure he was skeptical, despite his interest in psychic abilities. We talked about atmospheric conditions creating ghost phenomena and other pseudo-scientific nonsense for the entire break, and Pete and I both rejected Rob's collected logic.

"Just trying to be sure it's not nothing," Rob said.

I gave him one final "Well, we saw something!" and he seemed satisfied that we had encountered a real phantom.

Two days later, after he had been there at night again himself, Pete told me that Rob had gone to the graveyard with a 35mm camera containing infrared film—a tape recorder, too. Of course, the poor man came up with nothing. I wish I had known what night Rob was visiting the cemetery. He'd have seen *something*!

Pete and I then made trips to the archives of the Placentia Library, where a historian told us that the Pink Lady was a little girl's hallucination.

On another day, we went to an old pawn shop in Upland where poltergeist phenomena supposedly existed. I have to admit that I was glad we just drove by!

Later, we paid a visit to Pete's friend, Tim Edgerton in Upland. This visit was genuinely frightening. Tim told us an actual ghost had been seen many times in the old manor house, where he was caretaker. He had seen it. So had his girlfriend. We went there after dark, of course. Tim saw me staring intently as some ornate moldings in a bedroom upstairs and suddenly asked me "What are you looking at?" with a great deal of urgency in his voice. The ghost was unpredictable and he thought for a moment that I was experiencing some sort of paranormal event. Even though the atmosphere in the house was heavy and dark, Clara Lou Nisbet, the resident spirit, didn't put on a performance for us that night.

By now, our Missus had flaked off her screen and disappeared into the void of the garage. The combination of Freddy's scare-night man-handling and careless storage was too much for the paint. Soon, the last semblance of her existence, the painted cardboard backing (which I took great pains to hide on Pete's occasional visits), was skewered with sharp sticks pitched by Freddy's and my idle hands. It, too, was gone after a month.

It was now late December, and the hatred that had been growing between Pete and his roommates at the apartment they shared in Fullerton had reached a peak. When both roomies were at their respective parents' homes, Pete moved all his belongings out, and we had a field day. Dead fish here and there, eggy-weggs under the mattresses, Pepsi on the toilet seats, piss in the Sunny Delight—you name it. Vicious, callous fun to show that Pete could play the same kind of pranks he had long endured. My farewell card from Volt included the offering from Pete shown opposite.

And who do you think Pete shared a new apartment with in Anaheim? Why, me, of course! Over time, bad blood had been created between Virge and Freddy and me, so Pete and I leased a two-bedroom apartment, and I left the Filipos' without much ado.

I was reminded of the Pink Lady for another two full months before I would move on again… A dough-man drawing on Pete's floor, an old

note from Volt written in non-repro-blue ink, photographs Virge and I
helped Pete take at the Yorba Historical Cemetery just days after the scare.
Memorabilia of a fleeting shadow. A lady of my own creation, who, for
her brightest moment, sparked a keen interest in the spiritual for a poor
wretched soul. Pete would believe in the Pink Lady until he was disabused
by a mutual friend years later, and to this very day, when I reflect upon
that chilly night in October, I vividly recall my affair with the Pink Lady of
Yorba Linda. ■

The front of my Volt farewell card, drawn by Pete Scalzo (1981)

EPILOGUE

 I left Yorba Linda in January of 1981. After Freddy and Virge and I burglarized the Yorba Linda Middle School and I came close to inadvertently bringing the law down upon us, there was a quick decline in our friendships. I retired from the thievery-for-fun business. They thought I was a pussy, but I just couldn't take any more chances. And, the thrill was gone.

But, that didn't stop Virge and Freddy from breaking into a couple of pet shops during my final days at the Filipos' place. Pet shops! They meticulously disassembled the back door of one store and discovered that the owners were living in a room at the back. Their little dog was going ape-shit, making a huge racket, but the elderly proprietors didn't budge. They pretended to be asleep. No doubt they were afraid they would be murdered! Freddy and Virge robbed the place just the same. Unmitigated gall! Their gift of a three-foot ball python did little to make me enthusiastic about their bold and reckless new activities. I was beginning to see what Freddy and Virge had become: heartless common criminals with no common sense. I was happy to be rid of them when I moved on.

After I left Southern California in March of '81, Virge went on to have a job working the conveyor belts at a local Best Products* store—graveyard shift. He walked away with a shitload of sports equipment, including a compound bow. The management was eventually suspicious of him and had one of the nighttime employees pretend he was also a thief. This coworker asked Virge in confidence if he had any purloined goods for sale. Virge took the guy out to the parking lot after their shift and popped the trunk on his car. It was full of Best Products merchandise. Busted! A face-to-face meeting with management resulted in a deal. Best Products wouldn't prosecute Virge if he returned all of their crap. He did, and of course was fired. That was it. He walked away a free man and one lucky bastard!

It was around this time that Virge had a major falling out with Freddy and they parted ways forever.

It was through the grapevine—or maybe a little Internet bird told me—that I managed to get information about the players in this book as the years and decades wore on. Some of the information was firsthand.

After I returned to Southern California and was three years into my studies at Cal State Fullerton, I had brief contact with Virge. By 1985, Virge had found Jesus, and *this time* it was serious. He made a lame attempt at rekindling our friendship, which ended up being a ruse to save my soul. He was sure that I was still an unrepentant sinner. After all, I was cohabitating with my fetching and busty girlfriend at the time and this was at least a *venial sin*, and perhaps even a *cardinal sin*. He presumed that he could tell me how I should live my life, which involved dumping my girlfriend and pursuing a chaste existence. I'm sure part of this was just jealousy on Virge's part. Anyway, I gave Virge the old heave-ho after this little episode. I never saw him again.

I know for a fact that Virge dropped out of seminary school at some point between 1982 and 1985 (I'm sure Jesus was *not* pleased). I got this tidbit straight from the horse's ass's mouth. He also had a stint in the Navy where he mostly flew around in planes over endless tracts of ocean tracking submarines. His military experience certainly wasn't good, as he described his brothers-in-arms as, "The worst scum I ever met." Classic Virge.

Whether or not he went on to another learning institution is a mystery to me, though he may have had classes at Cal State Fullerton after the Navy. Google tells me that Virge eventually landed in San Mateo, about twenty miles south of San Francisco. He had some kind of writing job there. Perhaps the job involved casting judgments of some kind or another, which would have been a perfect fit for old Virge.

In 1982, I also had brief contact with Virge's brother, Jake. Jake had become the consummate pot-head. He was completely addicted to weed. He was so shameless about his use that his parents had basically thrown up their hands—they even turned their heads when Jake began to smoke dope in his bedroom whenever he desired. I know this because I shared a bowl-full with him there. Imagine a chain smoker and just replace the tobacco with cannabis. That's all Jake wanted to do. Smoke pot. Freddy and I should never have introduced him to the stuff. Regrettable. However, Jake did eventually get married and have a couple of kids. From what I've been able to learn from the Internet, he's currently in residence—or *still* in residence—at the family home in Yorba Linda that he and his brother occupied in 1980. I'm sure the place reeks of marijuana.

From what little I know about Freddy, he never went on to college. I suspect that he spent some time in a trade school or apprenticed with someone. He became a carpenter and furniture builder and had a shop in Hawaii for a while. He set up shop in Idaho sometime later. Not exactly the CEO of IKEA, but good for Freddy. Freddy was always good at building things. Even things that didn't explode.

Virge told me that shortly after I left the Filipos' place in 1981, Freddy filled doubled black plastic garbage bags with his precious power tools from Yorba Linda Middle School and buried them one night in the field up the street with the dead orange trees. When they retrieved them a few months later, they discovered that everything was rusted and unusable.

The Filipo property changed for the worse. Sometime in the '90s, Arnie and Midge sold the place. The land was subdivided, and the lovely custom ranch-style house soon occupied a patch of dirt at the top of the hill facing a fence and some shrubs that separated the old property from the new. No more was there a view of the lovely fruit trees, eucalyptus and pines. All of the trees were mowed down to accommodate the subdivision. Even the majestic Canary Island pine was brought down at some point. Like the vast majority of Yorba Linda, the property's charm and rustic appeal disappeared. The open fields near the Filipo property are long gone—victim to the spread of tract housing—enormous two-story houses with small footprints and tiny yards. No one wants to actually take care of a yard anymore, do they? Too much trouble. Smaller yards also mean more houses can be packed into a neighborhood. More money for the developers.

Pete Scalzo developed such an interest in the paranormal after his "ghost sighting" that he pursued video taping a documentary of locations in Southern California that had a reputation for being haunted. I had brief contact with Pete after starting college in 1982. He lived in an apartment complex that bordered the dormitories I lived in during my freshman year. Ultimately failing as a cinematographer, he went on to do jobs similar to the one he had at Volt.

Pete had become bitter, jaded, and mean. He treated me like a stupid younger brother, which I didn't deserve. My college roommates and I started referring to Pete as "Pete the Meat," and not because he had a prodigious pecker. This grew out of "Meatus Defeatus," a Latinesque phrase that we had coined to describe someone who was both a dick and self-defeating. I soon grew tired of Pete taking out his frustrations on me and we parted ways.

Pete's dream had always been to work for an animation studio. He did so at least briefly somewhere in the Los Angeles area. Somehow, Pete could never make a long-term go of it at jobs. According to him, the managers were always despicable or incompetent, the companies were conducting their business poorly, employees were systematically abused, or he was discriminated against because he looked too Asian. It was always someone else's fault. He was a victim of "The System." I learned about all of this through a mutual friend, Max.

Max had phoned Pete sometime in the 2000s to reconnect with him. Pete was very terse, and Max could hear a woman screaming at him from somewhere in the background. "I gotta go!" Pete suddenly announced. "Click!" Obviously, Pete continued to have the kind of luck with the ladies that he deserved. Max had earlier let him off the hook where the Pink Lady was concerned, too. According to Max, it went something like this:

> "After going up and down California with Pete looking for ghosts, he finally broke out one day and said he suspected that you had put one over on him… My eyes kept darting back and forth as I was trying to change the subject. 'Did you know about it?' he asked me. I hemmed and hawed and coughed a little and told him I really did have a belief in spirits… But, did I know about it? Uhhhmmm well… I think that sort of started an end to our friendship…"

Thanks, Max. I suppose it was long overdue, and Pete wasn't especially surprised.

As for me, I never again so much as nicked a Snickers bar after leaving Yorba Linda. Now, I'm old. I have the gray beard, thinning hair, arthritis, and high blood pressure to prove it. I was almost killed in a bad traffic accident in the San Joaquin Valley in November of 1981 (T-boned by a lumber truck), but I made a complete recovery. Afterward, I earned three degrees—both a bachelor's and master's degree in the visual arts, plus a diploma in web design and interactive communications. From 1991 to 2013, I worked as a graphic designer and senior communications specialist for a couple of large companies. Two long unemployed periods were thrown in to keep me humble. I experienced a failed marriage when I was in my twenties, but I've been happily married to a super-smart Polish doll since 2013. I'm now on disability for spinal osteoarthritis and semi-retired—and an author, evidently. Not bad for a former wrongdoer. (I must also mention that I've been subject to crime on a number of occasions. Theft to be precise. Karma is a bitch.)

So, Dear Reader, what's the moral to the stories presented in this book? What's the take-away—especially for someone in their late teens who has aspirations to become a red-assed baboon or is already acting like a red-assed baboon? Choose your friends wisely! Any kind of crime is bad, and repeated crime will eventually have ugly consequences. Don't deceive or defraud people—it can interfere with the course of their lives in unexpected ways and come back to "haunt" you. Nurture a conscience. Learn to put yourself in other people's shoes. Know that there will always be people who are smarter and more clever than you are. And, don't do your number-twos in inappropriate places or you'll get a terrible nickname like "The Phantom Crapper."

Parents take heed. Be involved with your teenager! You can prevent red-assed baboonism. Prankfurters evolve from poor parenting. Specifically, parents who aren't sufficiently involved with their kids, or simply have no desire to be involved with their kids at all. I know this for a fact. I had this kind of parenting, as did Freddy and Virge and Jake. Listen to your teenager. If you're curious about what's going on in their life, or something seems hinky, don't just ask questions, sit back and listen. Validate their feelings, show trust, don't be a dictator, give praise, control your emotions, do things together and share regular meals together. But, *not* incinerated plain hamburger patties topped with their own fat. It's disgusting.

In closing, if I may wax both religious and philosophical, our highest calling as spirits in the material world (if you believe in this sort of thing or simply like the song by The Police) is to love each other and help each other. Life is a test. Adversity is a test of our character. Put good things out to the Universe and good things will come back.

And you teenage kids out there! Steal, and you will be stolen from. Prank, and you will be pranked. Don't waste your short, precious time on this spinning rock being a crook or trickster or mean, dimwitted, garden-variety dick. A Prankfurter will pay strange, unexpected, and sometimes awful prices for their transgressions. ▪

MAPS

BASTANCHURY RD.

1980

THE FIELD

DRAINAGE DITCH

FIELD WITH
DEAD ORANGE GROVE

THE BIKE TRAIL

PRENTISS DRIVE

THE BIKE TRAIL

BERRY TRENCH

N

LOIE ST.

VERGE'S PLACE

LARO LN.

DRAINAGE DITCH

FIELD

MIMOSA DR.

FREDDY'S PLACE

EL CAJON AVE.

ROSE DR.

THE BIKE TRAIL

TENNIS
COURTS

GATE

ROSE DRIVE
ELEMENTARY
SCHOOL

UTILITY
ROOM

SUBURBAN SPRAWL: 1980 VS. 2019

Shown here and on the facing page are aerial
photographs of some of the places mentioned
in this book. These two images do well to show
how Yorba Linda has lost much of its charm.
While there were still open spaces in 1980,
every available square inch of free land had been
consumed by housing and businesses by 2019.
Although some would argue that suburban
sprawl has its benefits, such as creating economic
growth for a city, there's only so far that the
sprawl can go. Simply making neighborhoods
more densely populated has many negative
consequences for residents and the environment.

2019

THE FIELD

FIELD WITH DEAD ORANGE GROVE

DRAINAGE DITCH

THE BIKE TRAIL

PRENTISS DRIVE

N

LOIE ST.

VERGE'S PLACE

THE BIKE TRAIL

BERM TRENCH

LARO LN.

FIELD

MIMOSA DR.

FREDDY'S PLACE

ROSE DR.

EL CAJON AVE.

THE BIKE TRAIL

Virge's place (left) and Freddy's place (below) in 1980. Note the number of trees, particularly in Freddy's orange grove. The giant Canary Island pine is on the east side of Freddy's house.

The same properties in 2019. Freddy's former home occupies a dirt patch at the top of the hill. A subdivision built in the 1990s uses almost two-thirds of the original land.

TENNIS COURTS

ROSE DRIVE ELEMENTARY SCHOOL

UTILITY ROOM

(Photo: Google Earth - www.google.com/earth®)

GLOSSARY

110 camera 49

A cartridge-based film format used in still photography. 110 is essentially a miniaturized version of Kodak's earlier 126 film format. Frames are just 13mm × 17mm. Film processors for these formats of film are now almost nonexistent.

Best Products 189

A chain of American catalog showroom retail stores. Also known simply as *Best*. The last Best Products stores closed in 1997.

BMX 154, 168

Abbreviation for bicycle motocross or a bicycle designed for bicycle motocross.

California High School Equivalency Test ii

Students who pass this test verify their high school level skills and may leave high school early. Students receive a Certificate of Proficiency, which is equal by law to a California high school diploma.

Conyne Kite 83

A hybrid kite combination of a Conyne box kite and a Delta kite. The kite is very stable and flies well in a large variety of winds.

Day-Glo 55

A brand of bright fluorescent paint and pigments, such as those used in safety applications, artwork, and signage.

Doctor Demento 163

Barret Eugene "Barry" Hansen, an American radio broadcaster and record collector specializing in novelty songs, comedy, and strange or unusual recordings dating from the early days of phonograph records to the present.

Gallo 60, 61

A winery and wine distributor. The largest exporter of California wines. Famous for their giant 4 liter (1.05 gallon) wines in glass bottles. Maker of the low-end fortified wines *Thunderbird* and *Night Train Express*.

GMC Jimmy 67

A full-sized sport utility vehicle (SUV). The name was intended to make GM Jimmy sound similar to how Jeep was a pronunciation of GP in the competing market. Discontinued in 1991 and replaced by the Yukon.

Hairball 33, 119
Adj.: 80s slang word used to describe crazy situations or unbelievable circumstances.

Hans Holzer 128
An American paranormal researcher and author who wrote more than 120 books on supernatural and occult subjects for the popular market. Sometimes credited with having coined the term *ghost hunter*.

Instamatic 123, 184
An inexpensive, easy-to-load 126 or 110 cartridge-based roll film format camera. Film processors for this format of film are now almost nonexistent.

K-EARTH 101 101
KRTH 101.1 FM. A radio station serving the Greater Los Angeles Area. It currently broadcasts a classic hits format branded as K-Earth 101.

KMET 44
KMET 94.7 AM. A Los Angeles radio station which pioneered the"underground" progressive rock format. Nicknamed *The Mighty Met*. Defunct since 1987.

Loady 154, 155
N.: Slang for a person who is a habitual user of alcohol or drugs. Derived from the adjective *loaded*, under the influence of alcohol or drugs.

Mentally Gifted Minor (MGM) iii
A '60s and '70s special education program for children who were identified as gifted or talented. Currently known as G.A.T.E. (gifted and talented education).

Miller's Outpost 41
A clothing store chain. Became Anchor Blue in the late '90s and filed for Chapter 11 bankruptcy in 2009.

Nodding-Bird Oil Pump 22
A pumpjack. An overground drive for a reciprocating piston pump in an oil well. Its up-and-down motion and shape resemble a bird pecking at the ground.

Porta-Pad 49
A sturdy, plastic tripod model rocket launching pad by Estes, which assembles quickly and easily and can tilt up to 30 degrees from vertical.

Radical 17
Adj.: 80s slang word used to describe someone or something extreme. Often shortened to *rad*. Also another word for *cool, awesome, wicked*.

Reuben's Plankhouse i
A Coco's/Far West Services dinner house featuring steak and seafood. Now defunct.

Skaggs 79, 123
A food, drug, and retail goods chain. Became part of Albertsons, Inc. in 1998.

Sketch-Prone 116
Adj.: 80s slang word used to describe someone having a natural inclination to become scared or paranoid.

Skiod 116, 129
N.: 80s Slang word for *kid, child, youngster*. Usually used disparagingly. Often used in conjunction with *sketch-prone*, as in *sketch-prone skiod*.

Snag (Snagged, Snagging) 41, 44, 106, 110, 119,184
Vb.: To steal.

Solar Igniter 48, 51, 57
An Estes brand igniter (or electric match) which is electrically initiated and ignites the composite propellant in a model rocket engine. Currently known as Solar Starters.

Tolkienian 66
Of or relating to J. R. R. Tolkien or his writings, of which the best known are the fantasy epics *The Hobbit* and *The Lord of the Rings*.

Two-Backed Beast (Making The) 14
Vb.: A euphemism for having sex deriving from Shakespeare.

Wrist Rocket 14, 58
A powerful wrist-braced slingshot employing surgical tubing to provide power for the projectile instead of flat elastic bands.

ENDNOTES

[1]Sharon Okada, *Meet California's Most Conservative City*, The Sacramento Bee, Retrieved March 23, 2019. www.sacbee.com/site-services/databases/article204236199.html.

[2]Richard G. Porter, Jack Curry, Steve Reddicliffe, TV Guide Magazine, *50 Worst Shows of All-Time* (New York: TV Guide Magazine Group, July 20-26, 2002), 12. Print.

[3]Susan Gaede, *Anybody See a Pink Lady?* (Yorba Linda: Yorba Linda Star, June 19, 1980), 1. Print.

[4]Virginia Lamkin, *Yorba Linda's Pink Lady*, Seeks Ghost Blog, Retrieved February 24, 2019. www.seeksghosts.blogspot.com/2015/04/yorba-lindas-pink-lady.html.

[5]Aerial Maps, 1980. Aerials by Netronline. Retrieved April 22, 2019. www.historicaerials.com.

[6]Aerial Maps, 2019. Google Earth. Retrieved April 22, 2019. www.google.com/earth.

SUGGESTED READING

Chunder, M. Nelson, Hayduke, George, *Spite, Malice and Revenge: The Ultimate Guide to Getting Even (3 Diabolical Volumes in 1)* (Avenel: Gramercy Books, 1988), ISBN-13: 978-0517676042.

Jones, Sebastian A., *Parenting Teenage Boys: How to Form a Bond, Turn Problem Behaviors, Communicate and Listen to your Teenage Son* (CreateSpace Independent Publishing Platform, 2017), ISBN-13: 978-1975755355.

Myers, Arthur, *The Ghostly Register* (New York: McGraw-Hill Education, 1986), ISBN-13: 978-0809250813.

Ogden, Tom, *Haunted Cemeteries: Creepy Crypts, Spine-Tingling Spirits, and Midnight Mayhem* (Guilford: Globe Pequot Press, 2010), ISBN-13: 978-0762756582.

Tino-Sandoval, Cindy, *Images of America: Yorba Linda* (Mt. Pleasant: Arcadia Publishing, 2005), ISBN-13: 978-0738529622.

Made in the USA
Monee, IL
22 October 2023